Co**ntents**

Chapter 3: The Early Years 37

Chapter 4: Education 47

Introduction

- Are you the parent of a child with Down's syndrome?
- Are you trying to find out more about the condition?
- Do you support families of children with Down's syndrome?

f you are trying to piece together information about Down's syndrome, this practical guide is for you. It is full of information about Down's syndrome and packed with simple, useful tips to help you access services to effectively support your child, your family or the people you work with.

About Down's syndrome

Down's syndrome affects around 750 babies in the UK each year. This book covers all aspects of Down's syndrome – from diagnosis to adulthood. Read chapter 1 to get an understanding of the different types of Down's syndrome that exist, the characteristics and how it affects people. Chapter 2 explores antenatal screening and the diagnosis of Down's syndrome, including the impact it has on the family.

Education and health

When your child has Down's syndrome, education and schooling can be a huge worry. Chapter 3 looks at services available in the early years and explains about pre-school provision. Chapter 4 focuses on statutory education and guides you through the system.

Health matters are explored in chapter 5. Some conditions occur more often in people with Down's syndrome, this chapter explains about the most common conditions and the checks should that take place to minimise any problems.

Family life

Chapter 6 explores the impact that parenting a child with Down's syndrome can have on family life. It looks at how to support the other children in the family and strengthen your relationship with your partner. Sleep deprivation and challenging behaviour can make any parent feel stressed – chapter 7 looks at how to deal with these difficulties using simple techniques. Finances can become strained when a child has Down's syndrome, so chapter 8 examines the issue of finance and is packed with tips to help families make ends meet.

When you are a parent of a child with an additional need, you often find yourself in numerous meetings with professionals. Chapter 9 helps you to prepare for these meetings so that you get the questions answered that you need answering. Chapter 10 will help you and your family support your child's transition into adulthood. It may seem a long time away at the moment but it is never too early to start to plan.

Acknowledgements

Thanks for help with this book go to Dr Sharon Bowring, Johanna Payton and the Down's Syndrome Association.

Disclaimer

This book is for general information about Down's syndrome. Anyone with health concerns should consult their GP or healthcare professional in the first instance. This book can be used alongside professional medical advice but does not replace it – always check with your GP or healthcare professional before acting on any of the medical information in this book.

Particularly long terms have been abbreviated to their initials throughout the book, please make use of the acronyms page if you find you cannot remember what each one stands for.

Acronyms

ASD	Atrial septal defect
CVS	Chorionic villus sampling
DLA	Disability Living Allowance
IEP	Individual Education Plan
LA	Local authority
LSC	Learning and Skills Council
OSA	Obstructive sleep apnoea
SEN	Special educational needs
SENDIST	Special Educational Needs and Disability Tribunal
SENCO	Special educational needs co-ordinator
SLT	Speech and language therapist
VSD	Ventricular septal defect

1

What is Down's Syndrome?

Perhaps you've just found out that your unborn child may have Down's syndrome, or perhaps you have been living as the parent of a child with Down's syndrome for a number of years. Alternatively, you may work with children with Down's syndrome and want to find out more.

Whatever your situation, this chapter will give you the facts behind the condition. Most importantly though, people with Down's syndrome are in many ways like the rest of us. Their condition is only one aspect of their lives. Although this book talks about the condition and how it may apply to some people, it's important to remember every person with Down's syndrome is different.

In the past, people with Down's syndrome were put in 'long stay hospitals' or deemed ineducable, and were not given the chance to develop their abilities. Now, fewer and fewer people with Down's syndrome are in long-term care. Children with Down's syndrome have the right to an education in mainstream school, and there is more support so that they can develop their own skills, strengths and abilities. People with Down's syndrome are also able to get help and support to live as independently as possible in the community.

Despite this, some people with Down's syndrome and their families struggle to get access to the right care and the support that they need. By reading this book, you can develop your understanding of the condition and, perhaps more importantly, find out about the help available and how to access it. Read on to find out about what Down's syndrome is and how it happens.

Do you recognise someone with Down's syndrome?

Most people will recognise a child or adult with Down's syndrome. There is a characteristic set of facial features: a small nose with a wide bridge, low ears, a small chin and a round face. People with Down's syndrome also tend to be short and have learning difficulties.

Health and Down's syndrome

Some people with Down's syndrome have health problems including heart conditions, short- or long-sightedness and developmental disabilities. With good care, however, people with Down's syndrome can make the most of their abilities and live a happy life. Also modern medical care can help improve some health problems and prevent others developing.

Personality and Down's syndrome

In the past, people with Down's syndrome have been stereotyped as pleasant, happy, passive and compliant, but more recent research shows that this is a myth. Like people without Down's syndrome, people with the condition are all different and have different personalities. However, children with Down's syndrome can learn how to get on with people more quickly than they learn some other skills, which may be the basis for the stereotype.

One research paper found that adults with Down's syndrome are less likely to show behaviour problems than adults with other types of learning disabilities. People with Down's syndrome may appreciate routine as a way of feeling in control of their lives.

Development of a child with Down's syndrome

A child with Down's syndrome may develop an understanding of what is being said to them before they learn to express themselves through language.

Children with Down's syndrome will develop skills more slowly than other children, but this will vary enormously between individual children. Some may start walking at the age of two, while others may not walk until four. A physiotherapist can help a child with Down's syndrome develop their motor skills. A child's fine motor skills – their ability to pick up and handle small objects – are also likely to be delayed. Occupational therapy is used to help develop these skills.

A child with Down's syndrome may develop an understanding of what is being said to them before they learn to express themselves through language. Many will benefit from speech therapy to assist in developing linguistic skills. As people with Down's syndrome are more prone to ear problems, it is also important to check for hearing problems at this stage as recurrent infections and temporary hearing loss can slow speech development.

Learning and Down's syndrome

Down's syndrome causes learning disabilities: people with the condition have a lower IQ than the general population. The degree of impairment varies enormously between different people. Children with Down's syndrome can get on successfully at school if the best ways of teaching them are identified early on. Many benefit from some specialised teaching within a mainstream school.

What causes Down's syndrome?

Your body is made up of cells and each cell has a nucleus. Within the nucleus are 23 pairs of chromosomes which store your genes. Down's syndrome occurs when there is an extra copy of chromosome 21, which is why it's also known as trisomy 21.

It is not known what causes this extra chromosome. It may come from the mother or the father. The older the mother is, the more likely it is that an extra chromosome will occur and cause Down's syndrome in a baby.

There is a significantly higher risk of Down's syndrome if you are pregnant over the age of 35, but because many more women have babies under the age of 35, the majority of babies with Down's syndrome are born to women under 35.

Down's syndrome is not caused by anything a mother-to-be does during pregnancy or before conception. It occurs in all countries and does not depend on your race or ethnicity. The condition is named after a British doctor, John Langdon Down, who identified it in 1866. It was not until 1959 that the chromosomal abnormality responsible was found.

The effects of an extra chromosome can be very different in different individuals.

How common is Down's syndrome?

For every 1,000 babies born in the UK, one is likely to have Down's syndrome. The Down's Syndrome Association estimate that there are around 60,000 people in the UK with the condition.

Around 600-750 babies are born with the condition each year, but a significant number of parents decide not to go ahead with the pregnancy once they have a diagnosis of Down's syndrome.

Detecting Down's syndrome

The risk of Down's syndrome in an unborn child can be screened for at the end of the first trimester or during the early part of the second trimester – depending on the test at around 12-13 weeks or 15-20 weeks. The exact tests you are offered on the NHS will depend on where you live; you can also opt for private antenatal screening.

One routine test is known as nuchal translucency testing. During this test, a measurement is taken, via ultrasound, of the fold of skin at the back of the foetus's neck. Other tests involve taking a blood sample. Like all screening tests, these tests only indicate the chance of the condition and do not give a definite diagnosis. For every 20 women who are told that they have a higher than average chance of having a baby with Down's syndrome, one result will be a 'false positive'. This means that the test has suggested the foetus will have Down's syndrome when it does not.

Because of this, women are offered the chance to have further tests. An amniocentesis or chorionic villus sampling (CVS) involves taking a sample of cells from around the baby. These tests can give a more definite answer as to whether the condition is present, but they do have a slight risk of causing a miscarriage (see chapter 2 for more on this subject). *Pregnancy: Older Women – The Essential Guide* (Need2Know) contains extensive information on the tests available if your unborn child is thought to be at risk of Down's syndrome.

Before birth it is impossible to predict how an individual with Down's syndrome will be affected by the condition. Some people born with Down's syndrome will have a relatively high IQ and few health problems. Others will be more severely affected.

Some people born with Down's syndrome will have a relatively high IQ and few health problems. Others will be more severely affected.

Types of Down's syndrome

Regular trisomy 21

Generally, most types of Down's syndrome (around 94%) are due to regular trisomy 21, an extra copy of the 21st chromosome. People with regular trisomy 21 have mild to moderate learning disabilities, with an IQ ranging from 50-70 if mild and 35-50 if moderate.

Mosaic

In mosaic trisomy 21, only some of the cells in the body have the extra chromosome. This only occurs in 1-2% of people with Down's syndrome. People with mosaic Down's syndrome are likely to have a somewhat higher IQ.

Translocation

In around 4% of people with Down's syndrome, the extra chromosome 21 material comes from an abnormality in one of the parent's genes. Either parent, who will appear normal, may have the long arm of chromosome 21 attached to another chromosome. This can lead to an extra chromosome 21 being created during reproduction, producing a child with Down's syndrome. The child will have extra chromosome 21 material attached to another chromosome. This is also called Familial Down's syndrome and does not depend on the mother's age.

Characteristics of Down's syndrome

You may recognise that someone has Down's syndrome from their facial features. However, there are further, less visible results from the extra chromosome which are present to a greater or lesser extent.

Physical characteristics of Down's syndrome:

- Below average weight and length at birth.
- A small mouth and corresponding protruding or oversized tongue.
- Almond shaped eyes with an upwards slant.
- Recurrent ear infections.
- Low muscle tone.
- Learning difficulties.
- Short stature.
- Single crease on palms of hands (also called the Simian crease).
- Short hands.
- A larger than normal space between the big and second toes.

Health risks and Down's syndrome

People with Down's syndrome have an increased risk of:

- Thyroid dysfunctions.
- Heart defects.
- Gut problems including gastro oesophageal reflux disease.
- Obstructive sleep apnoea.

They may also develop Alzheimer's disease or dementia around 20-30 years earlier than people in the general population.

Less commonly, some people with Down's syndrome may have an increased risk of serious illnesses including:

- Leukaemia.
- Immune deficiencies.
- Epilepsy.

People with Down's syndrome have a lower risk of most kinds of cancer, hardening of the arteries and diabetic eye disease.

See chapter 5 for more details on these conditions and how they can affect some people with Down's syndrome.

People with Down's syndrome have a lower risk of most kinds of cancer, hardening of the arteries and diabetic eye disease.

What treatments are available?

Down's syndrome itself cannot be treated, but complications due to the chromosomal abnormality can be helped with appropriate medical treatment. As one example, someone with Down's syndrome is more likely to need glasses, and parents should watch out for ear infections. They may require heart surgery if they have certain heart defects.

People with Down's syndrome have a slightly shorter life expectancy, but they can live to around 60 years old.

Quick action checklist

This chapter has introduced you to Down's syndrome. You may want to:

- Find out more about testing for Down's syndrome by reading chapter 2.
- Learn about support and development in the early years in chapter 3.

More help

Further information about Down's syndrome can be obtained from the Down's Syndrome Association. Contact details for all organisations can be found in the help list at the back of this book.

Summing Up

People with Down's syndrome are all different and will have their own individual personalities.

Down's syndrome is caused by an extra chromosome which causes mild to moderate learning difficulties. Down's syndrome can be screened for during pregnancy – there is more about this in the next chapter.

People with the condition may develop some skills more slowly than others and need support to reach their full potential. There are also some health problems which occur more often in people with Down's syndrome than the general population.

Overall, though, each person with Down's syndrome can live a happy and fulfilling life with some extra help and support.

Finding Out Your Child Has Down's Syndrome

n this chapter we look at how you may find out that your child is likely to have Down's syndrome. In the UK there has been a pregnancy screening programme in place for more than 20 years, giving pregnant women the chance to find out the likelihood of their unborn baby having Down's syndrome. There are further diagnostic tests which are offered to women whose foetus has a high risk of Down's syndrome. No screening programme is totally accurate, so there are a number of babies born each year who were screened as low risk for Down's syndrome, yet were born with the condition.

Whether you are given a 'high risk' test result or only find out that your child has Down's syndrome at birth, you will experience a range of feelings. Read on to find out more about the tests and the rollercoaster of emotions you may go through.

Detecting Down's syndrome

Women are offered tests to screen for Down's syndrome in their unborn child at the end of the first trimester of pregnancy or during the early part of the second trimester. There are different tests available and which ones you are offered can vary depending on where you live.

Different tests

In some hospitals, women in the UK are offered a blood test in the second trimester. The blood test measures chemicals in your blood to find out the probability that the baby has Down's syndrome.

In other hospitals, women are offered a nuchal translucency test and blood tests. The nuchal translucency test takes place during an ultrasound scan. The radiographer measures the amount of fluid at the back of your baby's neck. Nuchal thickness is increased in conditions associated with chromosomal abnormalities, which includes Down's syndrome. The combined measurements of the blood tests and the nuchal translucency test can be used to work out the chances that your baby will have Down's syndrome. The nuchal translucency test is usually done at the routine 12 week scan, but it can work between weeks 10 and 14. The nuchal translucency test will also work if you are pregnant with twins or more, as it can suggest which baby is affected.

If you do not have this test in this time slot, there is another blood test which looks at three or four chemicals in your blood to work out the chance of your baby having Down's syndrome. Blood screening alone cannot establish the chance of Down's syndrome in a multiple pregnancy.

All the tests depend on an accurate estimate of how many weeks pregnant you are.

Your results

After your tests, you will be given a figure which tells you the risk that your unborn baby has Down's syndrome.

If you are told that you have a low risk of having a baby with Down's syndrome, this does not rule out the condition entirely. Many of the parents who contributed to this book did not expect to have a baby with Down's syndrome.

If you are given a high risk of having a baby with Down's syndrome, this does not mean that the condition is definitely present. You will be offered further diagnostic tests if your risk is between 1 in 2 and 1 in 249 (1 in 150 in some areas).

Screening or diagnosis?

It is important to be clear about the difference between screening and diagnosis.

Women are offered screening tests during pregnancy. These tell you the chance of your baby having a condition, but they cannot say for definite whether it will be present or not.

Everything possible is done to make sure that a test is as accurate as possible, but some people may be told that there is a high chance that a condition is present when it is not (a false positive), and some people may be told that their baby is clear of a condition when in fact it is present.

If your screening test shows that you have a high chance of a condition being present, you will be offered a diagnostic test which can rule out the presence of a condition or confirm that it is there.

Going through the experience of a high risk screening result can feel traumatic. It can be hard to make the decision about whether to have a diagnostic test, especially when the test has a small risk of causing a miscarriage.

Down's Syndrome Association information officer Susannah Seyman says: 'Ideally, gather information before you step on to the rollercoaster that is testing. Think, "If my test came back positive, what would I do?" If you wouldn't terminate, you may then decide against testing. Just make an informed decision.'

Adele says: 'I had a high risk result for my third baby. The result was 1 in 65. We had the option of an amnio[centesis] but never considered it due to the risk of miscarriage. We paid for a private scan to look for any Down's syndrome characteristics. From the scan it looked like we were having a "normal" baby, but there were never any guarantees until he was born.'

Ideally, gather information before you step on to the rollercoaster that is testing. Think, "If my test came back positive, what would I do?" If you wouldn't terminate, you may then decide against testing. Just make an informed decision.

Your risk and your age

The chance of having a baby with Down's syndrome increases as you get older.

An average woman of 20 has a 1 in 1,450 chance of a baby with Down's syndrome, but by the age of 40 this has increased to 1 in 85. If you give birth to a baby when you are 49, this chance has increased to 1 in 25 – but remember that this still means that there are 24 chances that your baby won't have Down's syndrome.

Your age at the birth of your baby	Your chance of a baby with Down's syndrome
20	1:1450
30	1:940
40	1:85

Comparison of models of maternal age-specific risk for Down syndrome live births.
(Source: JK Morris, NJ Wald, DE Mutton, E Alberman, Prenatal Diagnosis, 2003, vol. 23, issue 3, pages 253-8)

Further tests

If you have a higher risk of Down's syndrome as a result of screening or if you have had Down's syndrome detected in a previous pregnancy, your doctor or midwife will offer you the chance to have CVS or amniocentesis. These tests can give you a definite answer about Down's syndrome.

Both CVS and amniocentesis are invasive tests. This means that they involve going into your body and taking a sample of cells from around the baby or the placenta. There is a small risk of miscarriage with these tests.

If you opt for CVS, a fine needle is inserted either through your abdomen or through your vagina to take a sample of cells from the placenta. This can be done from 10 weeks gestation onwards. You may get a provisional result within one to two days which takes two to three weeks to confirm.

With amniocentesis, a fine needle is inserted through your abdomen to take a sample of the fluid around the baby which contains foetal cells. You need to be at least 15 weeks pregnant to have an amniocentesis. In some areas, you may get provisional results in a day or two, but the full results can take two to three weeks to come through.

Both tests take around 10 minutes and may feel uncomfortable. You won't need to stay in hospital overnight though. Experts currently say the risk of miscarriage is about the same for both tests and one woman in every 100-200 may miscarry afterwards, whether this miscarriage occurs due to the test or would have happened anyway is unknown. A few women have mild problems afterwards such as bleeding or leakage of amniotic fluid.

The tests may confirm that your baby does have Down's syndrome, but they can also show that it is not present.

Before birth it is impossible to predict how an individual with Down's syndrome will be affected by the condition. Some people born with Down's syndrome will have few problems. Others will be more severely affected.

Before birth it is impossible to predict how an individual with Down's syndrome will be affected by the condition. Some people born with Down's syndrome will have few problems. Others will be more severely affected.

Lucy says: 'After a normal 12 week scan, I had a threatened miscarriage at 14 weeks and during the scan was told that the baby had a cystic hygroma, which meant that it had a 1 in 2 chance of having a chromosomal defect. I was initially against undertaking any amniocentesis due to the risk to the baby, but my husband talked me round. He said that he would find it very stressful to spend the rest of the pregnancy not knowing what we were facing and, although he knew that I wouldn't be able to consider termination, he felt that it would be useful to know so that we could prepare ourselves. I had the amniocentesis, which was painful and unpleasant, at 17 weeks and found out that I was having a little girl with Down's Syndrome.

'I am so grateful now that I was aware of that before she was born as I was able to come to terms with it and find out all about the condition before she came. I was able to accept her completely for who she was. She is four years old now and an absolute delight. Her smile lights up a room. I have never once regretted my decision to continue with the pregnancy.'

Your decisions

You can choose whether to be screened or not. You can choose to have all the tests offered or just some of them.

If you are told that your baby has a high risk of Down's syndrome, you have further decisions to think about.

- You can choose to carry on with the pregnancy and wait and see whether the condition is present when you give birth.

- You can choose a diagnostic test which will confirm if the condition is present or not, but these have a small risk of miscarriage.

- If you find that your baby has Down's syndrome, you will want to think about whether to continue with the pregnancy or whether to terminate it.

What other women do

Across the UK, widespread prenatal testing for Down's syndrome has been around for about 20 years. This testing has led to a small fall in the number of babies born with Down's syndrome. Since 2000, the number of babies born with Down's syndrome has decreased by 1%, despite more women having a baby later in life when the chances of having a child with Down's syndrome are greater. Since testing was introduced, 9 out of 10 women who are told that their baby will be born with Down's syndrome decide to terminate the pregnancy.

Debbie says: 'I have a six year old boy with Down's syndrome. When I was pregnant with him, I had the quad blood test which returned a relatively low risk rate, so I did not pursue any of the other tests available. After his birth and finding out that he had Down's syndrome, the first few days went by in a daze. All I really remember was the consultant saying "For every statistic no matter what the one in ratio, there has to be the one". Initially, part of me thought that I wished we had progressed further with some of the other more diagnostic tests, especially as I was classed as an older mum at 33. But during my pregnancy someone said to me, "I didn't have any antenatal tests, because I didn't know if I could deal with the results". If I asked myself "What would I have done if I had found out that my son had Down's syndrome?", I couldn't honestly answer that question.

'With that in mind, and lots of discussions and sleepless nights, me and my husband made the decision to have the CVS if I became pregnant again, and we had already decided on the outcome if the test had come back positive. We felt that we needed to make the decision at a time when emotions and hormones weren't dominant, and when we could have more time to think through things more rationally. I was relieved when the test came back normal for my second son (at the age of 36) as we had decided to terminate the pregnancy otherwise, but it was a stressful few days waiting for the result and then wondering if I was going to miscarry. The decision to have the CVS was based on the reality of already having a child with Down's syndrome. We love him dearly but we did not feel that we could cope if we had another child with Down's syndrome, so the high risk element of the CVS was worth it.'

Making your choice

There is no easy way to make this choice. You and your partner need to talk through the pros and cons of your own particular situation. It can help to find out more about living with someone with Down's syndrome. This book is a great place to start and there is a list of organisations at the end that can help too.

Your midwife and consultant will be able to help you understand the medical choices you have available. Johanna Payton, author of *Abortion – The Essential Guide*, explains:

'Deciding whether or not to have an abortion is an entirely personal decision and you should never feel pressured by anyone. Whatever the reason for your termination, including Down's syndrome, your doctor can only advise you and talk through the pros and cons of an abortion – they cannot, and should not, make the decision for you.

'The type of abortion procedure you can have depends on how many weeks pregnant you are. Your doctor or consultant should talk through all the options with you, and in order to have the termination a second doctor is also required to agree that an abortion is in your best interests.

'Having an abortion when your pregnancy was planned, or very much wanted, can be a big emotional challenge and you should be offered lots of help and support to recover from your bereavement. The charity Antenatal Results and Choices (www.arc-uk.org) is the only national charity providing non-directive support and information to parents throughout the antenatal testing process. They can offer support and advice specifically for parents dealing with the aftermath of a loss after a diagnosis of fetal abnormality.

If it appears that your child may have Down's syndrome when he or she is born, the medical staff will carry out chromosome tests to get a definitive result.

'If you go ahead with a termination, you may also find it helpful to talk to a bereavement charity such as Cruse Bereavement Care (www.crusebereavementcare.org) or SANDS (www.uk-sands.org), the stillbirth and neonatal death charity.

'Many women choose to have a termination after discovering their baby has Down's syndrome. It is rarely a choice that is taken lightly, and you certainly don't deserve to feel bad or anxious, or be made to feel guilty by others, afterwards. Seeking reassurance from someone supportive can help you to overcome any continuing feelings of guilt or shame, but remind yourself that whilst feeling guilty is a normal and understandable emotion after any pregnancy termination, you made the best decision you could under the circumstances.'

If you want to find out more about termination, read *Abortion – The Essential Guide* (Need2Know).

Diagnosis at birth

Despite the screening tests on offer, a handful of parents each year discover that their baby has Down's syndrome only after he or she is born. If you are not expecting your child to be born with Down's syndrome, you or the medical staff may quickly spot that there is a chance of the condition because of the way the baby looks when he or she is born.

Lisa and her partner looked at their child a few minutes after he was born and saw that he looked like he had Down's syndrome. She says:

'Initially it was total disbelief and shock. It felt like a dream. I thought the pethedine was messing about with my brain. For a couple of days we kept going over the nuchal fold test results and saying to ourselves, "Perhaps they did the test too early or too late, perhaps our dates were wrong, why didn't we ask for further tests, was the person that did the scan incompetent?" We tried to keep these thoughts to ourselves and didn't actually start throwing wild accusations around. The shock remained for several days before I switched to thinking, "Right, this has happened, you have to just get on with it". It took two to three days to get a definite diagnosis.'

If it appears that your child may have Down's syndrome when he or she is born, the medical staff will carry out chromosome tests to get a definitive result. As Lisa's experience shows, you will have to wait a few days to get the results.

If you are in the position of having just found out that your baby is likely to have Down's syndrome, Susannah Seyman, information officer for the Down's Syndrome Association, suggests: 'Take it easy on how much information you try to gather at first. There is a lot out there and some may never be relevant to you. You may end up frightening yourself. There is a little baby that needs everything any other baby might need. Down's syndrome is only part of them.'

Lisa says: 'The midwives and paediatricians that we met in the first few days were the people we needed to be the most well-informed, supportive and positive. But they lacked information and were too busy to talk about our worries. Two midwives who had experience of children with Down's syndrome were lovely and gave us the time to tell us of their positive experience of children with Down's syndrome, and one of them went to great lengths to get information for us.'

Health problems at birth

If your child is born with Down's syndrome, there are some health problems that your medical team will be looking out for. Around 4 in 10 children with Down's syndrome have a heart defect; a specialist will check if this is an issue for your baby. All babies get their hearing checked shortly after birth – children with Down's syndrome are more likely to have hearing problems.

Babies with Down's syndrome tend to have low muscle tone which can cause problems with feeding. Ask for the contact details of your local breastfeeding counsellor if this is an area where you need help. La Leche League and the NCT both offer breastfeeding helplines. You can read more about health problems associated with Down's syndrome in chapter 5.

Your feelings

If you have just found out that your child has Down's syndrome, or have been given a 'high risk' result after antenatal screening, all sorts of emotions will be going through your head. These emotions will change and over the days and weeks to come you can feel grief, anger, worry and more.

Rollercoaster of emotion

Going through these emotions can be like experiencing a rollercoaster. Scope has devised a model to help you see your way through the different stages.

Shock

The first thing you feel may be shock. Few parents go into antenatal screening expecting to be told that their child has a high risk of Down's syndrome. If you have been through screening and have been told that you have a low risk only to find that your child has Down's syndrome at birth, the shock can be even greater.

Denial

It isn't always easy to take this sort of news on board. You may feel that on one level you are carrying on as normal. Some days you may feel like you are unaffected by the news, but this can swiftly change and things can feel overwhelming again.

If your partner seems unaffected by the news, they may be in denial. Allow them time to move through this phase, even if you are feeling very differently to them.

The Emotional Rollercoaster

You can move up and down the emotional rollercoaster

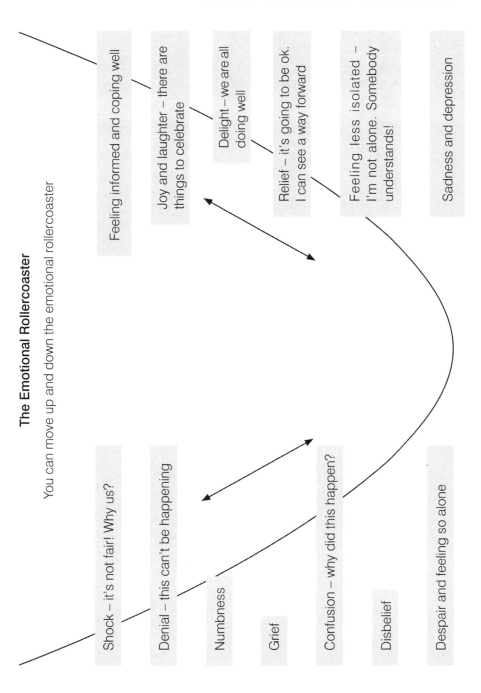

Feeling informed and coping well

Joy and laughter – there are things to celebrate

Delight – we are all doing well

Relief – it's going to be ok. I can see a way forward

Feeling less isolated – I'm not alone. Somebody understands!

Sadness and depression

Shock – it's not fair! Why us?

Denial – this can't be happening

Numbness

Grief

Confusion – why did this happen?

Disbelief

Despair and feeling so alone

(Source: adapted from 'Transitional Rollercoaster Model', published by Scope in 'Strengthening Families Training Pack', www.scope.org.uk.)

Numbness

If you feel like your situation is slightly unreal, or if it feels like it is happening to someone else, you may be feeling numb. Both numbness and denial can be helpful in one way as they allow us to keep on with the day-to-day necessities, but it can come as a shock when you move onto the next stage.

Grief

It is normal to feel grief when you receive a diagnosis. Many parents who have a child with Down's syndrome are very positive about the experience, but in the early stages you need to let yourself feel grief and sorrow. You may be mourning the ideas you had about your baby and adapting to a whole new set of ideas about what he or she will be like.

Confusion

The early days after diagnosis are often confusing. You will have been told that your child has a condition that you know little or nothing about. Professionals can offer you information which can seem overwhelming. Family and friends may ask questions that you don't yet know the answer to. Don't panic if you feel confused; as with all of these emotions, it is a stage that you will move through.

Disbelief

'Why is this happening to me?' is a question that many parents ask. You may want to check that the test results are correct, or keep looking at your baby to see if they really do look like they have Down's syndrome. It takes time for you to come to terms with a diagnosis of Down's syndrome.

Despair

At times you can feel despair and are unable to see a clear way ahead. Look after yourself at this time and remind yourself that things will improve.

Sadness and depression

At the bottom of the rollercoaster you can feel sad, depressed and alone. There is help and support available. Read on to see how things can improve and where to get help.

> Many parents who have a child with Down's syndrome are very positive about the experience, but in the early stages you need to let yourself feel grief and sorrow. You may be mourning the ideas you had about your baby and adapting to a whole new set of ideas about what he or she will be like.

Feeling less isolated – I'm not alone. Somebody understands!

The rollercoaster will eventually stop descending and you will be able to look at things in a more optimistic frame of mind. You may find support and make friends with other parents in similar situations.

Relief. It's going to be okay. I can see a way forward.

As you understand more about the condition, things can seem better. As you get to know your baby, you will bond and develop love for him or her, irrespective of any medical condition.

Soon you will be into the more positive phase of the emotional rollercoaster.

Delight. We are all doing well.

And some days, you will feel that it is just great to have your new baby as part of your family. The fact that they have Down's syndrome will just be part of them.

Joy and laughter. There are things to celebrate.

It may seem hard to realise this when you are in the initial phases, but having a child with Down's syndrome is in many ways like being a parent of any other child. You will relish and celebrate their every achievement, have fun times and enjoy time together as a family.

Feeling informed and coping well

On a day-to-day basis you will get back to taking everything in your stride.

Finally, don't worry if some days you feel worse, just when you thought you were coping well. You can go backwards on the emotional rollercoaster as well as forwards. Changes in your child's condition, news about new problems or any setback can leave you feeling down again. However, each time you travel the rollercoaster, you will gain more perspective and understand what is happening to your emotions, making it easier to ride out the low points.

Counselling and befriending schemes

Organisations like the Down's Syndrome Association have helplines (see help list for details), and they can also put you in touch with local support in your area. Your GP should also be able to help you find support and/or you may want to talk to a counsellor about what you are going through.

Quick action checklist

This chapter has talked about finding out that your child has Down's syndrome. You may now want to:

- Talk to your medical professional, midwife or GP about the screening and diagnostic tests for Down's syndrome and what they mean for you

- Read on to find out about living with a child with Down's syndrome and the support and help you can get.

- Call the Down's Syndrome Association to find out about the support they can offer and to be put in touch with your local group.

- Speak to your doctor or midwife about local counselling and support.

Summing Up

If you are pregnant, you can undergo screening tests to find out your chance of having a baby with Down's syndrome. Before you are screened, you may want to think about how you will feel if you receive a high risk result.

If the screening test shows that you have a high risk of Down's syndrome and you want a more definite answer, you can have an amniocentesis or CVS test. These tests do have a small risk of causing a miscarriage but can tell if your child will have Down's syndrome. Again, before the test, think what you might do if the result is positive, so you can be mentally prepared. Some parents only find out that their baby has Down's syndrome after he or she is born.

If you find out that your baby has Down's syndrome, you will go through a rollercoaster of emotions. Some days you will feel very down, but this does improve with time. Acknowledge that it is fine for you to struggle at times, and accept that your partner may have different feelings to you at different times. Ask for help and support from your GP or from a national or local Down's syndrome organisation.

3

The Early Years

Children learn a great deal during the early years of their lives. This chapter will look at how you can support your child with Down's syndrome to reach their full potential. It will help to guide you through the different agencies that you may come across that can help you and your child.

The first five years

Your baby may gain weight and grow more slowly than their peers. The Down's Syndrome Medical Interest Group has produced a growth chart for children with Down's syndrome which you may find useful. It shows the common milestones in a baby's life and compares at what age a baby with Down's syndrome will reach these milestones to other children. You can find this and other material at www.dsmig.org.uk. As with any child, you should consult a health practitioner if you have concerns about their wellbeing.

You may find that a child with Down's syndrome is more sensitive to different food textures and tastes. If you find that your child is having difficulties with feeding, it is important to consult a speech and language therapist (SLT) who specialises in feeding disorders.

Temperature regulation can be problematic for children with Down's syndrome so it is something that you need to be aware of. They can become overheated or cold far more quickly than their peers. Wearing layers can help them so that clothing can be reduced or added to quickly, and investing in a thermometer for their room so that you can monitor the climate can be very helpful to keep them comfortable.

Toilet training can take a little longer to establish for children with Down's syndrome. Your health visitor will be able to offer you support around this, and a consistent routine often helps children to get the hang of it, so try taking them to the toilet at the same times each day.

Children with Down's syndrome can follow an uneven pattern of development. They may appear to lose skills that they once had or suddenly develop skills in another area. They are particularly good at imitating others, so it is important that they have opportunities to socialise and watch others at play. You should take part in play sessions with your child and show them how to play with their toys and what each toy does. By modelling how to play, your child will learn what to do with the toys. The Early Support booklet Information for Parents: Down Syndrome gives lots of other ideas for things to do to develop your child's skills and is available free from the Early Support website (see help list).

Early Support

Early Support is a government programme which aims to improve the delivery of services to disabled children in the early years throughout England. The aim of Early Support is to keep parents at the heart of any discussion and decision making about their child, and is aimed at families of children under five years old.

There is also a developmental journal that has been produced specifically for children with Down's syndrome. The journal provides a place for the child's achievements to be recorded and celebrated while allowing areas that need additional support to be identified. You may well have already been issued with Early Support materials if you live in England, but if you haven't they can be accessed via the Early Support website. Those of you living outside England may also find it useful to look at the materials available online.

Portage

Portage is a home visiting service for pre-school children with additional needs. It was developed in the United States during the 1970s in an area called Portage.

Home visits take place on a regular basis in order to support parents to feel confident in developing their child's skills. Portage aims to make learning fun for all the family.

Leonora's son accessed the service. She tells us: 'The home visitor first came when our son was around seven weeks old. She encouraged us, loved him and gave us a good role model for communicating and playing with him. We found Portage a very useful service.'

There are currently around 150 services nationally and parents can self-refer if they feel it will be of benefit to their child. Details of the National Portage Society can be found in the help list.

Signing

Signing can be used successfully with young children that have Down's syndrome. They are often good visual learners and therefore they may be helped to understand more about what is said when it is supported by a sign. If your child learns to sign, it will help them communicate more efficiently.

Some parents are concerned that if they use signing, their child will be discouraged to speak. There is no evidence to suggest this is a problem. In fact, evidence suggests that children who use sign language are more likely to use speech than those who aren't signers.

Signing can be used successfully with young children that have Down's syndrome. They are often good visual learners and therefore they may be helped to understand more about what is said when it is supported by a sign.

Makaton

Makaton is a signing system that was developed in the 1970s and uses signs based on British Sign Language. Speech is always used alongside Makaton signs so that the child is hearing the word as well as seeing the sign.

Makaton symbols are also used to support understanding. Symbols are pictures that represent a word, for example a symbol of a cup may be shown to a child to reinforce that it is time for a drink. Symbols are used to develop early reading skills as well as to support understanding.

Makaton workshops are a good way for parents to learn Makaton – your SLT may be able to give you details of local workshops. Makaton also have a distance learning course for parents/carers, details of which can be found on their website which is listed in the help list.

Leonora's family found Makaton helpful: 'The whole family went on the foundation course, and his dad and I did courses all the way up to enhanced level. We paid for some of the courses ourselves and we had some for free because the local parent's group had raised money to pay for the course.

'I do think that it's worth investing in learning Makaton or some equivalent system, because this will help communication and will make parenting much easier. I would also recommend the Makaton Nursery Rhymes DVD with Dave Benson-Phillips.'

At first, learning Makaton may seem a little daunting, but with regular use you will quickly learn the signs. Using them on a daily basis with your child can help you to communicate more effectively with each other which can be very rewarding.

Signalong

Signalong is a system that is also based on British Sign Language and uses unaltered signs where possible. Again, Signalong is intended to be used alongside spoken language and has been designed for children who have language and learning difficulties. You can contact Signalong direct to find out more about their system (see help list).

Going to playgroup or nursery

All children learn through play, and children with Down's syndrome are no exception, but they may need a little more support in order to develop their play skills. You may decide that you want your child to access some form of pre-school before they start school. This can be an excellent way of developing their skills and helping them get on with children of their own age.

It can be a daunting task trying to find the right pre-school or nursery, yet many children with Down's syndrome will be able to access early years provision alongside their peers. Your local authority (LA) may have an early years inclusion teacher who is able to provide you with information regarding early years placements. Contact your LA's special educational needs department to find out if there is such a service.

It is important that you find out what provision is available locally – you may wish to consider a placement at:

- A childminder's home.
- A private nursery.
- A children's centre.
- A playgroup.

It is a good idea to visit the providers so that you can see what is on offer.

Lisa's son is eight months old now and has Down's syndrome. She shares with us her positive experience of childcare.

You may decide that you want your child to access some form of pre-school before they start school. This can be an excellent way of developing their skills and helping them get on with children of their own age.

'It was hard initially to find childcare because I thought we would need something special. But after visiting a few mainstream nurseries and childminders we found a nursery that just felt right. He loves going to nursery and they all love him to bits. He does lots of activities and they treat him like every other child. I can go to work and not worry about him at all.'

What to ask

Make up a list of things to ask at each place you visit. We've made some suggestions and left space for you to add your own questions.

- Do staff have any experience of working with children with Down's syndrome?
- Do staff have any experience of working with children with other additional needs?
- If your child uses sign language, can the staff sign or can they access training to learn to sign?
- What about food and eating – can they meet any dietary special needs?

You need to feel comfortable with the staff and assured that they are taking an interest in what you are telling them about your child.

My priorities

Take some time to consider what are the important things for you about an early years setting and list them opposite:

1 ....

....

2 ....

....

3 ....

....

4 ....

....

5 ....

....

Additional support

All children with Down's syndrome are described as having special educational needs. The setting that you choose will support your child's needs but at times they may have specialists visiting in order to give advice. The early years inclusion teacher may also be able to provide advice on how to work effectively with your child and monitor their progress. Therapists may also visit your child in their placement to offer advice to staff.

If your child is going to a nursery or pre-school, they will be placed on the Special Needs Register. If your child gets extra support when he or she is at nursery, the help is described as Early Years Action. If your child accesses help from people outside the pre-school such as therapists or specialist teachers, the help is described as Early Years Action Plus.

Special educational needs co-ordinator

Each pre-school or nursery should have a special educational needs co-ordinator, also known as a SENCO. The SENCO is the person in each pre-school, nursery or school who has responsibility for managing the special educational needs provision. It would be a good idea to ask to meet the SENCO when your child begins so that you can share with them what your child's needs are likely to be. The SENCO may share with you a document called an Individual Education Plan (IEP), which is used to plan and review your child's learning. The plan will set out small, achievable, measurable targets for your child and should be reviewed regularly. If your child's IEP hasn't been shared with you, ask staff whether an IEP has been put into place.

Statement of Special Educational Needs

Some children with Down's syndrome will require a Statement of Special Educational Needs from their LA, for example if your child is to attend a special school they will require one. The statutory assessment is carried out if your child needs a great deal of help or extra resources. The LA carries out the assessment and will ask specialists for advice about your child.

As a parent, you can write to the LA to request an assessment. Your child's nursery setting can also request an assessment but must consult with you first. More information about this process is given in the next chapter.

Starting school

Your child must begin school in the term following their fifth birthday, unless you choose to home educate. Many schools have 'foundation stage one' classes which mean that children can begin school when they are three years old. If your child requires a special school placement, they will usually be able to begin school on a part-time placement from the age of around two and a half.

Quick action checklist

Here is a quick checklist of actions to try next:

- Request Early Support materials if you do not already have these (see website).
- Contact your local Portage Service.
- Make appointments to view early years provisions for your child.

Summing Up

During the early years, your child will learn a great deal. This learning can be supported by accessing suitable provision and services to help them to meet their full potential. This is an exciting period in your child's life, where they will learn a great deal through play and socialisation. It is important that they access a stimulating environment where their skills can develop. It can also be a daunting time for you as a parent, but accessing local support groups can help you to feel less isolated. It is helpful to speak to other parents who have used local services and can give you positive feedback. Make sure that you ask other parents questions and also professionals that you come into contact with. The early years are a learning experience for you as well as your child.

Down's Syndrome Association information officer Susannah Seyman says: 'Call the Down's Syndrome Association and we can provide details of other families in the area who can be the best source of local information.'

Education

Finding your way around the education system can be challenging when your child has Down's syndrome. You will probably have many questions about where and how your child will be educated. You will encounter a number of professionals in the education service; our simple guide will help you to understand their different roles and how they can support your child.

This chapter will help you to understand about the different types of provision available. It will also help you to understand about statutory assessment for special educational needs and where to turn to if you need more support.

Special Educational Needs Service

Your LA has a section that is responsible for special educational needs. This service can provide additional support for children with Down's syndrome and their families; this support can include advice on your child's education and supporting their transition from one setting to another. This may also include advice on the setting that your child attends to ensure that they are meeting their full potential. If you are not accessing any support from the Special Educational Needs (SEN) Service, you should contact your LA to find out what is available locally. Alternatively, you may wish to speak to one of the professionals that is involved with your family and request that they refer your child to the SEN Service.

Mainstream or special school?

More and more children with Down's syndrome are being educated in mainstream schools with varying levels of support. It is often beneficial to your child to be educated alongside their peers, as children with Down's syndrome can thrive in an environment where they are provided with role models by other children.

Katharine's son is due to attend a mainstream school, here she tells us how she came to that decision: 'I chose the school in the same way that I did for my other child. I visited to have a look round but I mainly focused on the social aspect. We live in a small village and I wanted my son to go where the majority of people I know send their children, to make having friends easier for him.'

The government is committed to 'inclusion' which means that all children should be included fully in school life and access mainstream provision where possible. For inclusion to be successful, careful planning needs to take place between both parents and staff.

> More and more children with Down's syndrome are being educated in mainstream schools with varying levels of support.

Susannah Seyman, of the Down's Syndrome Association, says: 'Now children of primary school age almost all go to mainstream school and more and more are continuing in the mainstream for secondary school. This can really help your child feel part of the local community. A colleague's son recently left secondary school. He didn't have great academic qualifications, but there's not a night that goes by without someone knocking on the door and inviting him out.'

When trying to decide about the right educational setting, you may wish to consider the following points:

- How much support is your child likely to need during the day?
- At what particular times of the day are they more likely to need support? For example, lunch times, PE lessons, etc?
- Do the staff at your chosen setting need any additional training? For example, does your child use Makaton? If so, are the staff able to sign?
- How will the transition into the setting be managed? Will your child have the opportunity to visit the setting prior to starting? Will they be able to stay for a short time and then build up to a full session?
- Will staff from the receiving setting be able to visit your child in their current setting? This would help them to meet with staff who already know your child and find out about any strategies that they use to support your child's learning.
- How will the school communicate with you?
- Are there any specialist resources in place to meet your child's needs? For example, access to specialist teachers or therapists.
- What experience or training have the staff received about Down's syndrome?
- Would you feel confident leaving your child at this setting?
- Is the atmosphere warm and welcoming?

Some parents feel that a special school is the right option for their child. If you are unsure, it would be worth visiting a number of mainstream and special schools in your area. These visits can help you to meet the staff and to get a feel for the school. Special schools tend to take children with more particular special educational needs and often cater for children from the age of two to 19 years old. Your LA's special educational needs department will be able to inform you about local schools and what needs they cater for.

There are also a number of non-maintained special schools across the country. However, you should note that if there is a local state school that can meet your child's needs, the LA does not have to provide funding for your preferred school.

SEN Code of Practice

The SEN Code of Practice is a document that gives guidance to schools and the LA to help identify, assess and support children with additional needs. Processes and procedures that schools have to go through are set out in this document. You can request a free copy of this from the Department of Children and Families (see help list) if you would like to have a reference copy.

Additional support

Your child will be placed on the Special Educational Needs Register when they begin school to ensure that they gain the appropriate amount of additional support. If this support is provided solely by the school, it will be referred to as School Action. If the school needs specialist help from an outside agency to meet your child's needs, for example from an educational psychologist or specialist teacher, your child will be put on School Action Plus. If the school cannot provide your child with the help that they need, it may be necessary to consider asking for a statutory assessment for your child.

Statutory assessment

As we discussed in chapter 3, some children with Down's syndrome will require a Statement of Special Educational Needs from their LA, and all children attending a special school require a statement. The statutory assessment is carried out if your child needs a great deal of help or extra resources. The LA carries out the assessment and will ask specialists for advice about your child.

You can ask in writing for an assessment for your child. The Advisory Centre for Education (ACE centre) produces a template letter for parents to use which you may find useful (see help list). Your child's school or nursery can also request an assessment but must speak to you before doing so.

Statement of Special Education Needs

A statement will set out your child's needs and ensure that they receive the correct level of support. It is set out in six sections and will cover information such as your child's needs, any specialist help that is required and any non-educational needs that your child has. You will be sent a draft copy of the statement before the final version is written, and given 15 days to comment. You are entitled to disagree with all or part of it if you feel necessary.

If you don't agree with the statement you should:

- Speak to your named officer; you will be given their contact details at the beginning of the assessment process.

- Speak to your local Parent Partnership Service, further details about this service are to follow in this chapter

- Consider making an appeal to the Special Educational Needs and Disability Tribunal (SENDIST). Your LA will inform you of how to do this.

Individual Education Plans

IEPs, as they are more commonly known, are used to plan and review your child's learning. The plans set out small, measurable, achievable targets to support your child's development. They should be reviewed regularly and you and your child will be encouraged to work with staff to achieve the targets. You may wish to work on the set targets at home also.

Who can help?

You are likely to come across a number of education professionals during your child's time in school. The following list aims to act as a guide to inform you about who you may meet and what their roles will consist of:

- SENCO – a teacher who takes responsibility for the special educational needs provision in school. The SENCO, or special educational needs co-ordinator, will ensure that your child receives the correct level of support.

- Specialist teacher – teachers who are trained in specific areas to offer specialist support and employed by the LA. There are also specialist teachers for children with hearing and visual impairments.

A statement will set out your child's needs and ensure that they receive the correct level of support. It is set out in six sections and will cover information such as your child's needs, any specialist help that is required and any non-educational needs that your child has.

- Teaching assistant – teaching assistants work under the guidance of teachers. They may work with your child in the classroom or on a one-to-one basis to develop their skills.

- Educational psychologist – educational psychologists specialise in children's development and learning. Working alongside teachers and parents, they assess the child's psychological development to support learning and behaviour.

- Parent Partnership Service – your local branch will offer impartial information, advice and support to parents of children with special educational needs. They can advise you about who to speak to if you have concerns regarding your child's education. The service is free and confidential – see the help list for details.

Alex's son encountered difficulties when he moved from primary to secondary school. His advice to other parents is: 'Learn as much about special educational needs as possible and use the Parent Partnership Service.'

Your local Parent Partnership Service offers impartial information, advice and support to parents of children with special educational needs.

Quick action checklist

Here is a quick checklist of actions to try next:

- Develop good relationships with your child's setting.

- Look at the different types of provision that are on offer locally to ensure that you make an informed choice.

- Make use of the support services that are available to ensure that you are well informed. This will help you to make more informed decisions about your child's education.

Summing Up

Finding the right educational setting for your child can feel like a daunting task. Talk with staff regularly and if you have any concerns about your child's education, raise them immediately. Developing a good relationship with your child's SENCO will help you to feel more confident about raising concerns. Remember that you are the expert on your child and that it is important that your expertise is passed on to the education professionals. Parents have an extremely valuable role to play in their children's education and it is therefore important that you are well informed about what your child is doing at school.

Health Matters

5

I f your child is born with Down's syndrome, there are some health conditions that he or she is more likely to face than a person without the condition. Every person with Down's syndrome is different though, and some will have many health problems while others have very few.

- Leonora's son needs glasses. He has had speech and language problems, mobility problems and mild heart problems.

- Katherine's child had no health problems beyond a delay in developing gross and fine motor skills – that's walking, running, climbing and picking up small objects.

- Alex says his child has a lazy eye, speech and language problems, heart problems and is prone to constipation.

- Dora's child has speech and language problems along with minor problems with mobility.

This shows you the range of different ways people can be affected by Down's syndrome. In reading this chapter, bear in mind Dora's advice: 'When your baby is born, you read lots of literature that tells you such a percentage of babies with Down's syndrome have heart problems, they may have sight problems, etc. It is frightening, especially when you are trying to bond with your baby. Let me tell you, not every baby with Down's syndrome has these health problems and if they do develop something like glue ear or sight problems, they can usually be corrected. Speech will be delayed and it is important to make sure that you get regular speech and language input. Walking will also almost certainly be delayed, but your baby will get there. He or she will just go at his or her own pace – it is not a race.'

Most of the conditions that people with Down's syndrome are prone to can be treated; it may take persistence to get the correct treatment for some things, but people with Down's syndrome can live fulfilled and healthy lives with the right treatment. What's more, if your child has Down's syndrome, there are recommendations for the care they should get in their early years.

Most of the conditions that people with Down's syndrome are prone to can be treated; it may take persistence to get the correct treatment for some things, but people with Down's syndrome can live fulfilled and healthy lives with the right treatment.

What parents should expect

- Information about Down's syndrome before going home from hospital after the birth.

- A named person to contact if you have concerns.

- Therapists may become involved very early. For example, if there are feeding problems, you may see an SLT before you go home from hospital.

- An early appointment with a community paediatrician and regular reviews over the early years to monitor health, growth and development; to do blood tests for thyroid function annually until the age of five then every two years after that; to test for coeliac disease if suspected. These checks should continue until your child reaches 18.

- To see a physiotherapist in the first year at least until your child is walking and/or specific problems are resolved or to advise schools or nurseries about mobility issues.

- To see an occupational therapist in your child's first year to help with development of self care skills.

- To see an SLT about feeding issues and overall communication, which should continue into school and beyond.

- To have their eyes checked in their first few weeks of life, at 6-10 months, at 12 months, at 18-30 months, at four years and then every two years after that.

- To have their hearing checked at birth, at 6-10 months, annually until the age of five then every two years.

Therapy services are usually based in Child Development Centres, but most therapists will also see you at home and later in nursery and school.

Low muscle tone

People with Down's syndrome are born with low muscle tone, known as hypotonia. This can slow your child's physical development, but it also has implications for speech, digestion and breathing. Muscles in someone with hypotonia can seem less strong, respond more slowly or tire more rapidly.

Lisa says: 'My son has mild hypotonia but was sitting at eight months and stands with some support.'

Leonora's son needed a little help with his mobility which was easily provided: 'He pushed a trolley around for about four or five months, when he could nearly walk but not quite.'

Who can help?

A physiotherapist can help someone with Down's syndrome reach their full potential through providing physical intervention, advice and support to deal with many of the gross motor problems that can arise from low muscle tone. Gross motor development is all about helping your child sit, crawl, walk, run and jump. Physiotherapy can help your child to become more independent and develop their physical fitness.

Anything a physiotherapist does will work best if it is done in co-operation with you, your child's school and other professionals that help look after your child. Depending on your child's needs and the local services, you may see a physiotherapist at hospital or a clinic, and some may visit the school or your home. Your child's GP, paediatrician or other specialist doctor can refer him or her for physiotherapy.

Physiotherapy can help your child to become more independent and develop their physical fitness.

Low muscle tone can also make it harder for your child to develop fine motor skills, meaning the ability to co-ordinate their hands for detailed movement. This can make your child slower at learning how to feed or dress themselves. An occupational therapist can work with your child to help improve practical skills, working out ways to help your child maximise their potential in everyday life, from going to the toilet to holding a pencil or scissors.

With both physiotherapy and occupational therapy, any help will be given for a period of time and then your child's progress will be assessed. The therapist will explain to you if your child needs more therapy, would benefit from a break or has achieved their potential at the time.

Physiotherapists and occupational therapists need to be registered with the Health Professional's Council (see help list). You can find out more about occupational therapy and physiotherapy in Special Educational Needs – A Parent's Guide (Need2Know).

Heart defects

Unfortunately, 4 out of 10 children with Down's syndrome are born with a heart defect. This may be a small hole in the heart, also known as atrial septal defect or ASD. A hole means that the heart is less efficient and has to work harder to get blood round the body. It can lead to low oxygen in the blood stream being sent around the body and can cause breathlessness.

This condition was present in Lisa's son: 'His hole in the heart healed itself within six months.'

However, children can have more complex problems which will require surgery, but very few heart problems cannot be operated on.

All babies with Down's syndrome should be scanned in the early days after birth to check for heart problems. If you know before the birth your baby will have Down's syndrome, you may be offered a foetal heart scan while your baby is still in the womb.

The most common sort of heart problem, responsible for around 60% of heart problems in children with Down's syndrome, is complete atrioventricular canal defect. This consists of a large hole at the centre of the heart, located between the upper and lower chambers. A child with this problem is likely to be operated on at around three to four months old.

The next most common sort of defect is a ventricular septal defect (VSD), which is a defect in the wall dividing the right and left lower chambers of the heart. This is present in around three children in 10 with a Down's syndrome related heart problem. Some VSDs close by themselves but others may need surgery.

Around six children in 100 with Down's related heart problems suffer from something called tetralogy of fallot. The key issue with this is that all children will need surgery – the key problems are narrowing of the blood vessel that goes from the heart to the lungs at the point that it leaves the heart, and a hole between the two pumping chambers that allows blood to mix between the two sides of the heart.

Babies with this condition will have lower oxygen levels in their blood – their lips and tongue may look blue. Surgery can correct these usually without long-term problems – some babies will need two operations – the first a shunt to bypass the narrowing of the blood vessel to the lungs and then the definitive operation to correct the problem later in the first year.

For more about Down's syndrome and heart problems, get in touch with the Down's Heart Group (see help list).

All babies with Down's syndrome should be scanned in the early days after birth to check for heart problems. If you know before the birth your baby will have Down's syndrome, you may be offered a foetal heart scan while your baby is still in the womb.

Eyes, sight and Down's syndrome

People with Down's syndrome have eyes with a characteristic slanting appearance and a fold of skin, the epicanthal fold, from the nose to the inner eyebrow. There are some eye conditions that are more common in people with Down's syndrome than other people.

Around 20% of children with Down's syndrome have a squint, more correctly known as strabismus. This means that one eye is often used in preference to the other, and it can lead to a lazy eye (known as amblyopia). People with Down's syndrome are also more likely to need glasses.

In order to detect strabismus, long-sightedness, short-sightedness and other eye problems, it is important that anyone with Down's syndrome should have regular eye tests. Even pre-school children can have their eyes checked – treatment for a squint works best if started in the pre-school years, so it's good to start getting your child's eyes tested as early as you can. Children do not have to be able to talk to get their eyes tested and the NHS covers the cost.

Your child may have their eyes checked at their annual visit to the paediatrician. They should also have a check with an orthoptist and an ophthalmologist between 18 and 30 months of age. They will be invited for another check after their fourth birthday. Children will need their eyes checked regularly while they are growing, and your optometrist may advise that you come back every six months or annually. As an adult, eye tests should be carried out every two years.

Who can help?

Optometrist

An optometrist is trained to detect signs of eye disease and assess your child's eyes to see if they would benefit from glasses. Some optometrists are particularly interested in helping people with special educational needs or learning disabilities. Check on the Look Up website (see help list) to see if there is a practitioner near you.

Orthoptist

An orthoptist specialises in binocular vision, the way your child's eyes work together. They are usually hospital based and will help if your child has a squint or lazy eye.

Ophthalmologist

An ophthalmologist is a doctor who has gone on to specialise in eye disease. Some people with Down's syndrome can have other eye problems including:

- Blepharitis and conjunctivitis – an irritation of the eyelid edges. Eye infections can occur frequently due to poor tear drainage and the shape of the lids.

- Keratoconus – where the front of the eye is cone shaped rather than spherical. This causes blurred vision and may be treated with contact lenses.

- Cataracts – this clouding of the lens inside the eye can occur at an earlier age in people with Down's syndrome.

- Nystagmus – around one person in 10 with Down's syndrome has this condition which causes the eyes to flicker slightly, leading to poor vision.

If you think your child has any of these sight problems, your GP or optometrist will refer him or her to see an ophthalmologist.

Hearing and speech

People with Down's syndrome are more likely to have ear infections and some types of hearing loss because of the shape and structure of their ears and face. A slight hearing loss can hold back language development in children with Down's syndrome, increasing the effect of any learning difficulties.

As an example of the sort of problems that some children have, we hear from two parents.

Lisa says: 'My son has mild hearing problems which are just being monitored.'

Leonora says: 'My child had glue ear until he was 17 months old. He still gets occasional problems.'

Regular hearing checks

Most children born since 2005 will have their hearing checked soon after birth in the Newborn Hearing Screening Programme (www.hearing.screening.nhs.uk). Your child will then have a full review of their hearing between 6-10 months. Children with Down's syndrome should then have their hearing checked every year – during the check-up, the specialist should also check inside your child's ear at the same time to see the level of wax. Adults with Down's syndrome should have their ears examined every year for wax, and their hearing should be tested at least every five years. There are different tests which can be done depending on the person's development and ability to co-operate.

An audiologist identifies and assesses hearing problems and can recommend or provide ways to help and refer you to other specialist services.

Ear infections

People with Down's syndrome are more inclined to have persistent and ongoing ear infections, also known as otitis media with effusion or 'glue ear'. Their outer ear canal is narrow which makes it difficult for the ear to 'self clean', plus people with Down's syndrome tend to produce more wax. Sometimes people can find their ear is blocked as a result. Keep an eye on your child's ears, but do not try to clean them by putting anything in the ear canal. If your child keeps rubbing their ear or seems grumpier than usual, book an appointment with the GP to get their ears checked.

Hearing loss

There are a number of causes of hearing loss in people with Down's syndrome.

Wax blocking the outer ear, middle ear infections and glue ear can prevent sound travelling through the ear. Persistent untreated ear infections can also lead to scarring which damages hearing.

If hearing loss is caused by blocked ears, your GP may suggest that you use olive oil to soften the wax, and the GP can then remove it with a syringe. Antibiotics can help control persistent ear infections. If your child is diagnosed with glue ear, an operation to insert a grommet to help keep air flowing into the middle ear may be suggested. This operation won't suit everyone as some children's ear canals are too small to do this. Grommets can also fall out and need replacing.

The hair cells of part of the inner ear may be missing which causes deafness from birth. In other people, the hair cells deteriorate meaning that the person loses hearing as they age. This can start in the teenage years and many people with Down's syndrome will have significant hearing loss by the time they reach 40. This sort of hearing loss may be helped with hearing aids.

Hearing aids can help children with Down's syndrome and hearing loss develop their language skills. People with Down's syndrome tend to have small ears and will be offered small aids to suit them, and some people may find it's only possible to wear the aids for a limited time. Children may find a classroom FM system helps them hear better in class without needing to wear the aids. Speak to your school's SENCO to find out more about the options at your child's school and to get into contact with an advisory teacher for children with impaired hearing. See chapter 4 for more information about education.

From teeth to tummy

People with Down's syndrome have a slightly different skeletal structure and lax muscle tone which can lead to problems with speech, teeth and digestion.

The middle part of the face in someone with Down's syndrome is different to the rest of the population. Their tongue can appear to stick out more because it has a smaller space to sit in the mouth. People with Down's syndrome also often have enlarged tonsils and adenoids which can cause problems with breathing, particularly during sleep.

The mouth and teeth develop differently in people with Down's syndrome which can cause problems with suckling, swallowing, chewing and speaking. Without help, this can lead to permanent dribbling. Teeth can be small, missing or later to appear. Different people are affected to a different degree. A speech therapist can advise on activities that you can do to improve the way your child's mouth works.

Speech difficulties

Children with Down's syndrome have speech problems and delayed language development because of a combination of learning difficulties, low muscle tone, differences in their facial structure and sometimes hearing problems. On the plus side, children with Down's syndrome are usually sociable and good communicators.

Hearing aids can help children with Down's syndrome and hearing loss develop their language skills.

Start speech therapy early for maximum benefit. All the work done to develop their language and communication skills will help your child become independent and improve their quality of life. Your child will benefit from speech therapy throughout their life, but you may need to be persistent to get access – the Down's Syndrome Association can help with information on getting speech therapy.

An SLT can help your child develop their language skills. They will focus on communication and skills such as listening and turn taking. An SLT can also help you find out about signing with a system like Makaton, which can help your child communicate while they develop language skills. See chapter 3 for more about signing.

Who can help?

Speech therapy can start to work on non-verbal communication, listening and playing before your child is speaking.

An SLT is a health professional trained to diagnose, assess and treat adults and children with language, speech, voice, communication or swallowing disorders which affect their ability to communicate. Most work in the NHS, some offer private appointments and some work in schools.

You can contact an NHS SLT without getting a referral from your GP, and speech therapy can start to work on non-verbal communication, listening and playing before your child is speaking. Ask your local NHS trust for details of who to contact, or look at the list of SLT departments on ICAN's Talking Point website (www.talkingpoint.org.uk).

You will be given an appointment for an initial assessment. When you visit an SLT, they will assess your child's communication skills, speech and how they make speech sounds, the words that they use and their level of understanding in relation to their age and development. They will also look at how your child plays and communicates with others.

If your child struggles during the assessment, the SLT will take a break or stop altogether. The SLT is trained to get the best from your child, and in a few cases may recommend you come back to complete the assessment.

At the end of the assessment the SLT will explain whether your child needs any of the following:

- Help to develop a better understanding of words.
- Help with making speech sounds.
- Help with the words they are using.

You should also get a written report in the post.

The SLT often suggests activities for you and your child to do at home. Your SLT may ask you to bring your child in regularly, once a week or once a month, to help develop skills that are necessary for good speech, language and communication development. Sessions may be with your child individually or in a group of children working on similar issues. Due to waiting lists, there may be a delay before this can start. A group may meet for six weeks at a time, followed by a break to allow your child to consolidate the skills they have learnt.

The work you do with your child at home is almost more important than the sessions with the SLT, simply due to the fact that you spend so much more time with your child. The SLT may liaise with your child's school too so that work can be continued in class. If you have a pre-school child, ask the SLT to link up with pre-school services such as Portage or a community nursery nurse to help you carry on relevant activities at home. There is more about Portage in chapter 3.

Diet and digestion

People with Down's syndrome are likely to have digestive problems because either their organs are formed differently from usual, or because part of their digestive tract does not work properly. Watch your child to see if they have pain or are distressed after feeding as this may be an early sign of digestive problems.

Growth and feeding

While children with Down's syndrome do tend to grow more slowly than other children, sometimes weight loss or poor weight gain can be a sign of digestive problems. There are now growth charts available for children with Down's syndrome. They are available to buy in packs of 20 from www.dsmig.org.uk, or ask your health visitor or GP if they have them available.

Children with Down's syndrome may have problems co-ordinating sucking and swallowing from birth. Your health visitor, specialist nurse or SLT can help you work out the best way to help your baby to feed.

Reflux

Babies with Down's syndrome are more likely to have reflux, also known as gastro-oesophageal reflux disease. In this condition, food that has already passed into the stomach and beyond is vomited back up. Babies are more prone to this problem as they spend more time lying down and the muscle at the top of the stomach is yet to become strong. Different medicines can help by stopping the stomach contents flowing back, by neutralising the acid in the stomach and by helping the stomach muscles move food along. Very occasionally surgery is needed.

Internal blockages

Around one child in 10 born with Down's syndrome will also have a problem with the structure of their small bowel or pancreas. If there is a blockage, it may show up on the ultrasound before the birth. If not detected before birth, it can cause vomiting. Your child will be examined and x-rayed and any major blockage will be operated on swiftly. Sometimes children with Down's syndrome are born without an anal opening which also requires an urgent operation. In other cases, the opening may be narrow which can lead to a tendency to constipation.

Hirschprung's disease

A very small number of children with Down's syndrome, around 2%, are born with Hirschprung's disease. In this condition, part of the bowel wall is missing the nerve cells and therefore cannot push digestive matter along. This can lead to chronic constipation, poor weight gain, vomiting and a swollen abdomen. It is treated by surgery to remove the affected part of the bowel.

Coeliac disease

Another, small, group of children with Down's syndrome may have coeliac disease, an allergy to a protein found in wheat, known as gluten. People with coeliac disease can experience poor growth, diarrhoea, and excessive tiredness and lack of energy. All this can be improved with a gluten (wheat) free diet. Speak to your GP about getting a diagnosis before changing your child's diet.

Gum and dental issues

People with Down's syndrome are more prone to gum disease, which can lead to changes in behaviour, refusal to eat or swallowing food whole. They may be more likely to gag or vomit when being checked by the dentist.

Other health problems

Sleep apnoea and breathing difficulties

Large tonsils in young children with Down's syndrome can mean that they have sleep apnoea, temporary pauses in breathing while they sleep. This can lead to your child waking frequently in the night, something you may be unaware of if they settle themselves back to sleep. This can cause daytime sleepiness and lack of energy. It is worth talking to your GP about this – they may suggest removing the tonsils and adenoids or a referral for a sleep study to see if this is a problem for your child. See chapter 7 for more on sleep.

Cervical spine instability

Some people with Down's syndrome have a tendency to have a weak joint at the top of the spine. It is not possible to identify this problem in advance, but if your child needs surgery or is in an accident, the medical staff need to take extra care when moving their head while they are unconscious. Some activities are more high risk, so you may want to talk to your GP before your child takes part in gymnastics or other activities where they may land on their head.

Leukaemia

Children with Down's syndrome have an increased risk of developing leukaemia. In around 10% of newborns, there is a condition called transient leukaemia with raised levels of white blood cells which disappears on its own without treatment in just a few weeks or months. Some research has indicated that 3 in 10 infants with this sort of leukaemia go on to develop a different sort of leukaemia within the next three years. It is not clear why people with Down's syndrome have a higher chance of developing leukaemia but it seems to be linked to the extra chromosome.

Thyroid disease

People with Down's syndrome also have an increased risk of developing thyroid problems. The thyroid, a gland in the neck, helps regulate a person's energy levels. People with Down's syndrome can have an overactive thyroid, which can make a person agitated and jittery, but are much more likely to have an underactive thyroid. This leads to weight gain and lethargy, and slow physical and mental reactions.

Lack of thyroxine is a problem in around 15-20% of adolescents with Down's syndrome. This can be treated by taking a thyroxine tablet every day. Blood tests to check thyroid function will be done routinely through childhood

Alzheimer's disease

People with Down's syndrome also have an increased risk of developing Alzheimer's disease. Symptoms of Alzheimer's disease include:

- Loss of memory.
- Poor concentration.
- Difficulty finding the right words.
- Diminishing understanding of what others are saying.
- Problems remembering time and place.
- Difficulty with self-care, problem solving and domestic tasks.
- Mood changes and behaviour changes.

Almost everyone with Down's syndrome will develop the tangles and plaques in the brain that are associated with Alzheimer's disease, but not all of them will have symptoms. By 50-59 years of age, around 1 in 3 people with Down's syndrome will have some signs of Alzheimer's, rising to over half in the 60-69 age group. It can be hard to spot the early stages of Alzheimer's in someone with Down's syndrome as the person may find it harder to express how they feel that their abilities are changing.

You can help someone with Down's syndrome and dementia by keeping to a daily routine and developing visual reminders for both day-to-day activities and about the person's life story. There is also some medical help available – ask the specialist doctor whether drug treatment might help the person with Down's syndrome and dementia.

More help

Susannah Seyman, Down's Syndrome Association information officer, says: 'You can see this long list of health concerns and that can really scare you. Be positive. The medical profession know that these conditions happen more often and can check for them. The Down's Syndrome Association has a protocol on which tests your child should have at which age.'

Sometimes it can be frustrating when you know or suspect your child has a health problem. It can take persistence to get a diagnosis and the help they need. Join a support organisation to get help from other parents who have been through similar experiences and can recommend good sources of help. The right help can make an enormous difference to your child.

Leonora says: 'When [professionals] take the trouble to get to know him and his strengths and his difficulties, and they apply patience and skill, they get him doing all sorts of things I never would have expected.'

Quick action checklist

This chapter has explained about some heath problems experienced by people with Down's syndrome. You may now want to:

- Find out more about specific health problems.
- Talk to your GP or specialist.
- Get in touch with relevant support groups – see the help list for some suggestions.

Summing Up

People with Down's syndrome have a higher risk of some health conditions. Heart conditions will be checked for in the womb, at birth and within the first few weeks of life. You should get support from an early stage with feeding from an SLT.

If you are caring for someone with Down's syndrome, you will find that they have frequent appointments, particularly as a child. Regular reviews to monitor health, growth and development should continue until your child reaches 18.

Regular checks on hearing and sight are important too, as people with Down's syndrome are more likely to have hearing and sight problems. Fortunately, once detected, these can almost always be remedied.

You may find it confusing with lots of health information to take on board. You should be given a named officer to talk to about health concerns before your new baby leaves hospital. Once you are past the early stage, make sure you stay in touch with the GP, who can help you navigate through the necessary checks.

There is a lot that can be done now to make sure that the effects of these conditions are minimised, and people with Down's syndrome can live happy, healthy and fulfilled lives.

6

Enjoying Family Life

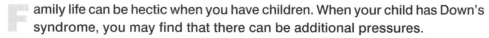

Family life can be hectic when you have children. When your child has Down's syndrome, you may find that there can be additional pressures.

Having a child with an additional need may impact on siblings and other family members. There can also be an impact on your relationship with your partner. Accessing support groups can be a helpful way to meet others in a similar situation.

Juggling everyday life can be difficult. In this chapter we provide simple, easy to follow tips to make family life easier and more enjoyable for everyone.

Siblings

It is not unusual for siblings to experience feelings of jealousy, particularly if a child has an additional need and therefore requires more attention.

Leonora's six year old son has Down's syndrome. He has an older sister who is 21 years old and an older brother who is 23 years old.

Leonora says: 'My daughter is now working with children with complex needs, and is studying psychology. I believe that she went down this career route because of her experience with her little brother. My eldest son finds it hard to come to terms with the slowness of his little brother's toilet training and general delay in acquiring skills. Both elder siblings get jealous of the way he always gets first priority; the disruption to the household routine, such as always making sure certain doors are closed and locked.'

It is not unusual for siblings to experience feelings of jealousy, particularly if a child has an additional need and therefore requires more attention. The following tips may help:

- Ensure that you spend time on a one-to-one basis with your other children regularly. If you have a partner, could you ask them to babysit your other child so that you can have some uninterrupted time together?

- It is important that you acknowledge your other children's feelings about their sibling. Listen to them when they explain how they feel.

- Siblings often want to know about medical conditions and may want to learn more about Down's syndrome. Offer to explain information to them in a way that they can understand.

- Grandparents may be a useful source of support for siblings. Would it be possible for them to spend some time at their grandparents' home on a regular basis?

- Meeting other siblings in a similar position can be helpful. Enquire locally as to whether there are any siblings groups available. Your child's school, health worker or social worker may be able to provide details.

- Siblings learn new skills as a result of having a sibling with Down's syndrome. These should be celebrated.

Karon has three sons aged six, four and two years old. Her middle son has Down's syndrome. Karon tells us about her positive experience with the boys: 'My eldest son is aware of other people with Down's syndrome, for example if he sees them on the television. He also knows some Makaton which I think is useful. My youngest son has been brought up in a signing household and uses many signs to communicate; I think he has benefitted from this tremendously. He is of a similar ability to Joe now and we call them the "twins" even though they are two years apart. They play together a lot.'

Susannah Seyman of the Down's Syndrome Association says: 'When I've spoken to the parents of new babies, often their other children have grounded them, saying things like, "He's my brother, whatever." Relationships with siblings are usually very normal, with the regular amount of squabbling. On the positive side, research has shown that lots of siblings go into social care professions.'

Sibs is a UK charity for those that grow up with a disabled brother or sister. The organisation aims to enhance the lives of siblings by offering information and support. Contact details for Sibs can be found in the help list.

Dads

While things are improving, support for dads can still be difficult to access. Many dads are working and find that they cannot always attend meetings or support groups in the day. However, it is important that dads do have the opportunity to talk to others about how they are feeling and any concerns that they have.

The Internet can be a great source of information and can be accessed 24 hours a day.

Many dads are working and find that they cannot always attend meetings or support groups in the day. However, it is important that dads do have the opportunity to talk to others about how they are feeling and any concerns that they have.

If you cannot get to an important meeting, ask for the contact details of the professional so that you can email or telephone them to discuss any issues that may arise.

Ensure that you have at least one person that you can speak openly and honestly to about your feelings. This may be a friend, colleague or your partner.

Contact a Family have a 'Dads' Zone' on their website; their contact details can be found in the help list.

Parental relationships

Having a child can change any relationship beyond recognition. Having a child with Down's syndrome can strengthen a relationship yet can also put the relationship under significant strain.

It is important that as a couple you make time for each other, even if it is just 10 minutes each day. The key to a good relationship is communication. It is important to spend time talking to each other on a daily basis. Physical contact such as a hug, holding hands or a foot massage can help you to feel reconnected to each other.

If you feel that your relationship is under pressure or breaking down then you may wish to consider counselling. You may wish to speak to your GP who can arrange for you to see a local counsellor.

Respite care

We all deserve a break and respite care can allow you to take some time off from caring for your child. You may have family members who are willing to look after your child for a few hours so that you can have some leisure time. Alternatively, you may need to explore other options. If you are receiving higher or middle rate Disability Living Allowance, you may be eligible for respite care from your LA. Your social worker will be able to advise you about what is available in your area.

Karon tells us: 'Both my children go to a childminder one day a week and I could not survive without that day to myself!'

Holidays

Holidays are supposed to be a time of fun and relaxation, yet they are also one of the most stressful times of the year for many families. Katharine explains: 'In your own home you are aware of all possible dangers, on holiday everything could be a problem; you have to be on guard 100% of the time.'

Leonora tells us: 'There are challenges that have to be dealt with. For example, the special diet means that we have to carry a refrigerated bag. At one place that we stayed they offered him the gluten-free bread and he got ill because it probably had buckwheat in it. A regular toilet is too high, so we need to take a footstool. Safety has to be managed and we have to check for hazards such as ponds and swimming pools in strange places. Managing a child who has no sense of danger can be difficult, particularly when you aren't quite sure where the next hazard is going to appear. Having said all that, our son is particularly easygoing and pleasant-mannered, so it is fun going out with him while we are away and seeing how he sets out to be friends with everyone.'

If you are feeling daunted by going away, you may wish to consider holidaying at a purpose built centre. There are a number of organisations that offer breaks to families who have a child with a disability. Contact a Family produce a guide entitled Holidays, Play and Leisure which outlines the details of where you can access short breaks (see help list).

Support groups

Support groups can provide parents with a tremendous amount of help. Olivia tells us: 'I find attending support groups extremely helpful. Getting together with other parents helps you to find out what services there are. Support groups also help to reduce your feelings of isolation and you realise that you are not the only one going through problems.'

Many schools now run support groups for parents of children with additional needs. A number of local support groups have their own websites and it would be worthwhile spending some time on the Internet to find out if there is anything in your area. The local library may be able to inform you of any support groups that are currently running, or call the Down's Syndrome Association for local contacts.

Scope provides a befriending service called Face2Face. The service is for parents of children with additional needs irrespective of diagnosis. The aim of the service is for parents to receive emotional support from other parents – there are trained befrienders who have been through an intense training programme in order to be able to offer a listening ear. As well as offering this service in areas across the country, they also offer an online service which can be helpful if you are working or if you just don't have time to meet up with a befriender on a regular basis. For details about the scheme, please see the help list.

Karon gives other parents the following advice: 'Join your local Down's Syndrome support group and get out there and meet other families. Also, if you can, join the DS-UK email group as there will almost certainly be someone on there who has words of wisdom for any concerns you might have.'

DS-UK provides informal support, information and discussions for both parents and professionals caring for a child with Down's syndrome. You can subscribe to the group by emailing listserv@listserv.down-syndrome.net and putting 'subscribe DS-UK' in the message.

Celebrate the good times

We are all guilty at times of forgetting to celebrate the successes that we and our children have. It is important to take time out not only to celebrate your child's achievements, but also to celebrate your own achievements as a parent.

Alex tells us that having a child with Down's syndrome was a positive life changing experience: 'Now I work for a disabled children's charity, I have started a ski club for disabled children and I'm involved in many voluntary groups, all as a result of fathering a child with Down's syndrome.'

More help

Making life easier

You may wish to follow the tips below to help make life easier on a day-to-day basis:

- Fix a whiteboard in your kitchen so that you can write down what needs to be done each day and who is supposed to be doing it. This makes sure that the whole family knows what is going on.

- Use a family calendar so that all appointments, work shifts and school events can be seen for each month.

- Put the alarm on for 10 minutes earlier each morning to avoid rushing around.

- Divide up family chores so that everyone has a part to play.

- Set up a folder containing letters about medical appointments so that you don't lose them.

- Eat at the table with your family on a regular basis and listen to each others' news.

- Keep family photos on the fridge to remind you of the fun times.

Susannah Seyman, Down's Syndrome Association information officer says: 'It is up to you to get the balance right and this can be hard, especially in the early days. Try to make time for every member of the family, including yourself.'

Quick action checklist

This chapter has highlighted the impact that having a child with Down's syndrome can have on family life. You may want to:

- Talk with other parents who have a child with Down's syndrome via a support group or the Internet.

- Find support for your other children, through family members and/or sibling support groups.

- Spend some time thinking about your family life and ways that you could improve it.

- Have you identified who you can share concerns with?

- Are your other children's emotional needs being met?

- Have you and your partner set aside some time for you to talk and to strengthen your relationship?

Summing Up

Family life can be stressful at times, yet it can also be very rewarding. It is important that you spend time talking with your partner and siblings about their feelings. It is also important that you have someone to speak to and that you form a support network around yourself.

Looking after yourself should be a priority so that you are then in a position to look after the other members of your family. If you find it difficult to talk to your family about how you are feeling, you need to make sure that you have some emotional support from another source, perhaps a friend or a parent in a similar situation.

Don't forget to celebrate the good times. It is all too easy to get bogged down with the things that are going badly and forget about what is going well.

7

Beating Stress, Sleeping Well

Being a parent can be incredibly stressful. When your child has Down's syndrome, your stress levels may be raised further. In this chapter, we examine what causes your stress and offer suggestions to help you to relax and manage your stress more effectively.

Sleep deprivation can lead to high stress levels. Many children with Down's syndrome have sleep difficulties. If you are one of the families that are suffering from broken nights' sleep, this chapter will help you to identify ways of improving the situation and making daily life easier.

Finally, dealing with challenging behaviour can be extremely stressful. In this chapter, we will outline some simple ideas to use with your child.

What causes you to feel stressed?

If you take care of your own wellbeing, you will be better placed to take care of your child's needs. What one person finds stressful another may not – we are all individuals. It is important to identify what causes you to feel stressed.

Karon tells us: 'Trying to fit in as many activities and therapies as I want to, or can afford, leads to me feeling stressed. You constantly want to do the best for your child and not let them down. Sometimes it just isn't possible to do everything that you want to. It can be incredibly difficult trying to fit in appointments and therapies.'

Cheryl suggests making a 'to do' list: 'I find making a list of things that I have to do is incredibly helpful. It keeps me focused on what needs to be done and I get a lot of satisfaction from crossing jobs off. I also review the list and see if all the jobs really need to be done. I'm not as hard on myself as I used to be and realise now that there is only so much that I can do during the day.'

James tells us that he gets stressed by worrying about the future: 'I start to think what will happen to Max when he starts school. How will he cope? What about when he grows up? Who will care for him if I'm not able to? All these thoughts lead me to feel very stressed. I've now joined a support group where I've met other parents who can really understand what I'm going through and sharing our experiences has really helped me to feel less stressed.'

In order to reduce your stress levels, you first need to identify what is making you feel stressed. Take some time to consider the three things that are making you feel most stressed in your life right now and write them opposite:

1 ....

....

2 ....

....

3 ....

....

If you have been able to identify what is causing you to feel stressed, you can take some positive action to reduce the levels of stress that you are experiencing. Consider what you can do in order to minimise the stress that each scenario is causing you. Think what advice you might give someone else in the same situation.

Perhaps you are too close to the situation to be able to see how to move forwards. You may wish to consider counselling so that you can share your stresses with a professional – talking about stress can be very therapeutic. If you feel that your stress levels are high and leading onto depression or anxiety, you should consult your GP for advice immediately.

For more information, see *Stress – The Essential Guide* (Need2Know).

Relaxation

It is vital that you have some relaxation time in order to keep your stress levels down and improve your overall health and wellbeing. It can be difficult to find time to relax when parenting, but it is important that you set aside at least 10 minutes each day to unwind. Some of us have a hobby that we find relaxing such as sewing or reading. Others may enjoy a bubble bath or listening to music. Relaxation should be an enjoyable experience, so if you aren't enjoying this time, perhaps you need to rethink it and try a different activity.

All of the following activities can be carried out at home: circle any that you may find relaxing and try to fit them into your schedule.

Gardening	Playing board games	Making craft items
Watching television	Baking	Listening to the radio
Listening to music	Meditation	Phone calls to friends
Knitting	Reading	Surfing the net
Sewing	Taking a bath	Writing letters

Now you need to set aside at least 10 minutes each day to enjoy your relaxing activity.

Top tips from other parents

We asked other parents of children with Down's syndrome for their top tips to avoid stress. Here is a selection of what they shared with us:

- Set the alarm for 10 minutes earlier, it helps to avoid those manic mornings.

- Write everything down; get a family planner up in your kitchen so that the whole family knows what the schedule is for the week. This way you won't miss appointments.

- Always allow 15 minutes more than you will need to get to appointments.

- Be prepared to wait at appointments, and pack a bag with toys and snacks for your child.

- Remember: what doesn't get done today will wait!

Sleep

Bedtime

If you are finding that your child has sleep difficulties, you are not alone. It is estimated that half of all children with Down's syndrome have sleep problems. Children with sleep difficulties are likely to display more challenging behaviour than those that are well rested, they are also less likely to meet their full potential. Parents who are sleep deprived are more likely to feel irritable and suffer from stress and depression.

It is very common for children's behaviour to impact on sleep difficulties. This is the same for all children, not just those with Down's syndrome. Children may display some of the following behaviours:

Tantrums around bedtime

- Unwillingness to get into bed and stay in bed without a parent being present.
- Insistence on sleeping in the parent's bed.
- Inability to settle to sleep without a parent being present.
- Repeated waking during the night and disturbing the parent.

Many of these problems are a result of the child not having learned to settle themselves to sleep. It is important that your child learns to go to sleep by themselves so that when they wake up during the night they can fall back to sleep without needing you. It is usually best to take a gradual approach to this. If you currently lie on your child's bed while they fall asleep, you should sit by the bed. Each night you can move nearer towards the door.

It is important not to give your child attention once you have said goodnight. Do not engage with them and avoid making eye contact. They need to learn that once it is bedtime the fun and games have finished for the day!

A good bedtime routine can help to minimise behavioural difficulties around bedtime. Do not let your child watch television or play computer games for an hour prior to bedtime as these can be mentally stimulating. Instead, opt for quiet activities such as colouring in or completing jigsaw puzzles. A bath is also a good way to aid relaxation; your child should not re-enter the living room after their bath but go straight to their bedroom ready for bed.

You may wish to give your child sensory indicators that bedtime is imminent. For example, the use of a certain bubble bath with a particular smell can help to set the scene. You could also play the same piece of calming music at the same time each night to give your child some sense of time. In contrast, you could use a rousing piece of music to indicate when it is time to get up in the morning.

Obstructive sleep apnoea

Obstructive sleep apnoea or OSA is more common in children with Down's syndrome than in the neuro-typical child. This is because of the physical traits associated with Down's syndrome including:

- Enlarged tonsils.
- Enlarged adenoids.
- Floppy throat muscles.
- Smaller airways.

OSA occurs when the airway at the back of the throat becomes blocked during sleep. When this happens, the child is woken up as they have difficulty breathing. These episodes can occur hundreds of times throughout the night, causing the child to have a poor sleep quality.

Signs of OSA include:

- Snoring.
- Coughing during sleep.
- Choking.
- Excessive sweating.
- Unusual sleeping position – the child may try to sleep with their head tilted back in order to open up their airways.
- Restless sleep.
- Interrupted breathing patterns.

If you suspect that your child may be suffering from OSA, seek medical advice. A full assessment will need to be completed and an overnight sleep study is often required in order to make a diagnosis.

Support for sleep

If you feel that you need support with sleep difficulties, you can contact your GP initially to find out if there are any specialist services in your area.

Scope runs a national support service called Sleep Solutions. The service is offered free of charge and families can benefit from working with a qualified sleep practitioner, who will work in partnership with the family to develop a sleep programme.

Karen Hunt, Sleep Solutions' national strategic development manager tells us: 'We work uniquely with both parents and practitioners at prevention, early and complex intervention levels. This is achieved through individual family work and group workshops tailored to the needs of parents and/or practitioners to facilitate positive change in sleep patterns.'

More information about the sleep service can be found in the help list.

Challenging behaviour

Managing challenging behaviour at home

Children with Down's syndrome may demonstrate more challenging behaviour than other children of the same age. Their behaviour can be magnified because of their limited communication skills, so it is important to establish clear boundaries for your child as early as possible.

Children with Down's syndrome will show the same behaviours as any other child. The key to managing the behaviour is to use positive reinforcement and to remain consistent. Praise your child when they are behaving as you want them to; some children may respond well to a reward system such as a star chart or stickers. Where possible, you should try to ignore any challenging behaviour so that your child will learn that they will get your attention when they are conforming.

Use your child's name at the beginning of sentences and use minimal language. For example, instead of saying 'Don't hit your sister, you will hurt her, Sam', simply state 'Sam, no hitting.'

Managing challenging behaviour outside the home

It can be incredibly stressful managing difficult behaviour outside the home. John tells us: 'I can cope with managing Chloe's behaviour at home, but when we are out and about I do find it more stressful. I'm aware of other people staring if she has a tantrum, which makes me feel like my parenting skills are being judged.'

While it isn't easy, do try to remain calm. Some parents find carrying business sized cards in their pockets that explain that their child has a special need can help. Handing them out to people who stare or make comments can be a helpful tool to distract them from your child's behaviour.

Quick action checklist

Here's a quick list so that you can identify areas that you need to work on:

- Have you identified ways that you can relax and make time for yourself on a daily basis?

- If your child has sleep difficulties, have you been able to identify any strategies to use?

- Have you set clear boundaries to your child regarding your expectations around behaviour?

Summing Up

Parenting is a stressful job, so it is important that you identify some time when you can relax, as sleep difficulties and challenging behaviour can impact on your stress levels. Sleep deprivation can lead you to feeling depressed and unable to cope. Make sure that you have somebody to talk to about how you are feeling and don't be afraid to ask for help either from members of your family, friends or professionals.

Susannah Seyman, Down's Syndrome Association information officer, says: 'Sleep is a big subject. A lot of new babies with Down's syndrome are very sleepy, but it doesn't stay that way. Children often have very disrupted sleep patterns. Talk to your GP to find out about sleep clinics and get help with conditions like sleep apnoea, which is more common in people with Down's syndrome.'

8

Finance

Caring for someone with a disability can have a big effect on the family finances. You may find that you are at home full-time when you had expected to be able to work. There can be additional costs such as transport to hospital, or you may find that your child needs specialist equipment. It can cost up to three times more to bring up a child with a disability.

One mum whose child has Down's syndrome has found a whole range of extra costs. She says: 'Childcare costs more and is harder to get. There were things to take him to every week: physio and swimming, and other appointments: podiatrist, paediatrician, eyes, ears. So it was harder to find work that fitted in to that timetable. It had to be near nursery because I had to be reliably there to collect at the end of the day, and sometimes I got delayed at the start of the day, so there was only "lunch lady" left as an occupation, and the money wasn't great. And even "lunch lady" I couldn't do on Wednesdays because he had his physio appointments then. He was ill for rather more time than the average child, and he had to take more time out of school/nursery when he was ill. So I didn't manage to get paid work.'

If you've found that your plans to work have had to change, and the costs of caring are adding up, read this chapter to find out about benefits, grants and other ways to keep your family finances in balance.

> Caring for someone with a disability can have a big effect on the family finances. You may find that you are at home full-time when you had expected to be able to work.

Benefits

Start by checking whether you are getting the benefits that you are entitled to. Susannah Seyman, Down's Syndrome Association information officer, says: 'We employ two welfare benefits advisers to help you make sure that you are getting everything that you are entitled to. They have a fund finding database and can help fill in disability learning allowance forms. They can even assist you with an appeal.'

Here is a quick summary of some relevant benefits.

Tax credits

Tax credits are payments from the government. If you are not getting tax credits, claim as soon as possible because they are normally only backdated for three months.

Child Tax Credit

This is for anyone who is responsible for at least one child or young person who normally lives with them. Your child should be under 16, or 16-19 and in education or training, or 16-17 and registered for work or training with the careers service or Connexions, Ministry of Defence, Department for Employment and Learning (in Northern Ireland) or an Education and Library Board (in Northern Ireland).

Working Tax Credit

This is for anyone who works but earns low wages.

Tax credits are based on your income in the previous tax year: a tax year runs from April to March. If you live with someone as a couple, you need to make a joint tax credits claim by filling in a claim form. You can order a tax credits claim pack from the Tax Credit Helpline (see help list). If you need help to fill in the form, speak to someone on the helpline, visit your local Jobcentre Plus or ask at a Citizen's Advice Bureau. The government advise that it can be worth claiming even if you suspect that your income is too high right now but may go down in future months. Tax credits will be affected by other benefits.

You may be able to get Disability Living Allowance (DLA) for someone with Down's syndrome if they need help with personal care or have walking difficulties.

Disability Living Allowance

You may be able to get Disability Living Allowance (DLA) for someone with Down's syndrome if they need help with personal care or have walking difficulties. For a child to get these benefits, they must need a lot more help or supervision than other children of the same age. Children usually only get benefit paid from the age of three months.

DLA – care

Personal care means that the person needs help with things such as washing, dressing, eating, getting to and using the toilet or communicating. Someone who needs supervision to avoid putting themselves or others in substantial danger or someone who is over 16 and unable to cook for themselves would also qualify for the care component of DLA. There are three rates of the care component:

- The lowest rate is for someone who needs help or supervision for some of the day or is unable to prepare a cooked main meal.

- The middle rate is for someone who needs help with personal care frequently or supervision continually throughout the day, or help with personal care or someone to watch over you during the night.

- The highest rate is for someone who needs help or supervision frequently throughout the day and during the night.

DLA – mobility

There are specific guidelines about when you can claim for the mobility aspects of DLA for a child. You can claim for mobility needs from:

- Age three, if your child is unable, or virtually unable, to walk.

- Age three, if your child is severely mentally impaired with severe behavioural problems and qualifies for the highest rate of care component.

- Age five, if your child needs guidance or supervision when walking out of doors.

If someone you care for is entitled to the mobility component of DLA, they can apply for the Motability scheme which helps disabled people buy or lease a car at an affordable price. If you care for a disabled person who does not drive, they can still apply to buy or lease a car through the scheme with you as their driver. You can also apply for a car on behalf of a child aged three or over.

You can find out about claiming DLA and ask for a claim pack through the Benefit Enquiry Line (see help list), via your local Jobcentre Plus, or download one online from www.direct.gov.uk. If you make a successful claim for DLA, this can also boost the amount you get through:

- Income Support.

- Pension Credit.

- Housing Benefit or Council Tax Benefit.

- Working Tax Credit.

- Child Tax Credit.

Carer's Allowance

You may also be able to get Carer's Allowance if you are aged 16 or over and spend at least 35 hours a week caring for a person who gets DLA at the middle or higher rate for personal care. Claiming Carer's Allowance can affect the level of some other benefits and entitlements that you, or the person you care for, receive. However, if you are claiming Income Support and you are also entitled to Carer's Allowance, you may be able to get an extra amount included in your Income Support. Plus, claiming Carer's Allowance entitles you to have your national insurance contributions paid. The phone number for Carer's Allowance is in the help list – you should contact them for a claim form.

Child Benefit

Child Benefit is a tax-free payment that you can claim for your child. It is usually paid every four weeks. The payment does not depend on your income or savings. You may be able to get Child Benefit if:

- Your child is under 16.

- Your child is over 16 and in education or training that qualifies for Child Benefit.

- Your child is 16 or 17, has left education or training that qualifies for Child Benefit and is registered for work, education or training with an approved body.

Find out more by calling the Child Benefit Helpline on 0845 302 1444.

Education Maintenance Allowance

This is for families that have a 16-17-year-old still in education. Your child's school or college should be able to give you details about making a claim. Receiving this allowance will not affect your other benefits.

Finding out

If you are unsure whether you are getting everything that you might be entitled to, you can call the Down's Syndrome Association welfare benefits advisers (see help list). The staff will check to see if you are missing out on anything.

There are other funds that can help you cope with extra costs of looking after someone with Down's syndrome. There are various ways to find out more about these funds. The charity Turn2us can also help you access any money that might be available to you through benefits, grants and other help. The Directory of Social Change publishes a book called A Guide to Grants for Individuals in Need, which

If you are unsure whether you are getting everything that you might be entitled to, you can call the Down's Syndrome Association welfare benefits advisers.

contains information on national and local charities that contribute to individuals in need. See if your local library has a copy, and contact your local organisation for carers as they will also know about funding available.

More help with finances

Family Fund

The Family Fund helps low income families with severely disabled children. Alex, father to a child with Down's syndrome, says: 'We've had help with a washing machine, a dryer, part funding for a trike and our holiday.'

The fund is available for families in England, Northern Ireland, Scotland and Wales and can be used for anything to make life easier and more enjoyable for the disabled child and their family, such as washing machines, driving lessons, hospital visiting costs, computers and holidays. The Family Fund is a registered charity, helping around 50,000 families in the UK with £30.5 million in grants a year. The amount of grant that you could receive will depend on your circumstances and the funding available when you apply. You can apply once a year, but the Family Fund will be flexible in cases of emergency or crisis.

To apply you must fill in an application form – contact details can be found in the help list.

> **The Family Fund is a registered charity, helping around 50,000 families in the UK with £30.5 million in grants a year.**

Social care

Social care can offer families additional financial support in exceptional circumstances. If you are in a difficult situation and face a problem like eviction or having your power supply cut off, contact your local social care department to see if they can help.

Debt

If you are in debt, start by making a list of what you owe. You need to prioritise paying debts for essentials first; this includes rent or mortgage payments as well as payment for heat, light and food. Try to move debts with higher interest rates to a lower rate and pay as much off as possible to clear the debts.

Talk to a trained adviser at a reputable organisation like the Citizen's Advice Bureau or the National Debtline. They can help you prioritise and negotiate payments so you can pay back a small amount that you can afford each month.

Help with short breaks and more

At the time of writing, money has been set aside to fund short breaks for families with a disabled child, and breaks can last from a few hours to a week. Your child could be cared for in their own home or given opportunities to access activities and places in the wider community. Contact your LA to find out about what is available in your area. There is also funding available through primary care trusts for short breaks, wheelchairs, community equipment and palliative care for children – ask your GP about what is available locally to you.

Cutting the cost of healthcare

If you get benefits or have a low income, you may also be entitled to free prescriptions, dental treatment, eye tests and help with the cost of travel to hospital. You can find out more about this in a booklet available from Jobcentre Plus offices, NHS hospitals, doctors, dentists, pharmacists and opticians. Ask for form HC11 – 'Help with Health Costs'.

Flexible ways to earn

There are various ways to earn money even if you have caring responsibilities. You could look for home-based work such as:

- Selling online through auction websites like eBay or even setting up your own online store.

- Signing up for a direct selling or party plan business that allows you to work flexibly.

- Offer a service from home – this could be anything from typing and ironing, to dog walking or pet sitting. You may be able to use specialist skills from previous employment or look into retraining.

- Becoming a mystery shopper – you will get paid to visit local stores and file a report.

You could also think about other ways to boost the family income by:

- Taking in a lodger.
- Offering accommodation to language students in vacation time.

For more ideas, look at www.familyfriendlyworking.co.uk. Bear in mind that any additional money you earn may affect your benefits and you should check with the HMRC about tax liability on any self-employed income.

Making a will

Making a will is one way to make sure that your assets are used to benefit your child. Setting up a trust can help ensure that your child can also receive benefits.

If you have a child with Down's syndrome, you will want to make sure that they are well cared for in the future. Making a will is one way to make sure that your assets are used to benefit your child. Setting up a trust can help ensure that your child can also receive benefits.

Many parents of children whose learning disabilities mean that they will need help to manage their money make arrangements for a discretionary trust. One or more trustees are appointed to manage any money or property and use the income to benefit the trust beneficiary, your child. The details of the trust will set out how the income should be used. Because the assets in the discretionary trust do not belong to your child, they are not taken into account when your child's entitlement to benefits is assessed.

Mencap offers a list of solicitors who have a specialist interest in creating wills that provide for the future of someone with a learning disability. You can send off for this through their website, www.mencap.org.uk.

Your next steps

Here is a quick checklist so you can check what action to try next:

- Take a benefit check to make sure you are claiming everything that you are entitled to.
- Look into ways to earn money from home-based work.
- If you are in debt, take some positive action and contact an adviser and begin to plan your way out of debt.
- Make a will that takes into account the needs of your child.

More help

Abilitynet offers advice on computers and software for children with a disability. They can advise on financial assistance from charitable trusts for equipment (see help list).

Disabled Living Foundation produces factsheets about children's daily living equipment. These can be downloaded from their website or you can call the helpline (see help list).

Summing Up

Caring for someone can stretch your budget, so make sure that you are getting all the benefits you are entitled to.

Several organisations can help you find out about benefits and grants. Contact the Down's Syndrome Association or Turn2Us for help. Look into the Family Fund for grants that can be used for anything from household equipment to a holiday.

Don't let debt get you down. Take control by listing your debts and talking to someone at the Citizen's Advice Bureau about affordable ways to repay them over time.

Look into flexible ways to earn while you are also a carer. This can help boost your income, but find out how much you can earn before your benefits are affected.

9

Working with Professionals

As the parent of someone with Down's syndrome, you may find that you and your family now come into contact with a wide range of professionals. When your child has an additional need, there are often numerous specialists involved including occupational therapists, specialist teachers, medical staff, SLTs, physiotherapists and the list goes on.

This chapter will explore how to work successfully with professionals so that you get the best outcome for your child. Attending meetings can be a daunting experience; our simple tips will help you to feel more confident and to get your point of view across successfully.

Discussing meetings with your partner if you have one, prior to them taking place, can help you to both feel more relaxed and to be clearer about the outcome that you would like.

It is important that you are aware of the role of each professional you're in contact with. If you are in any doubt, ask when you meet with them what their role involves and how they can support you and your child.

Professionals that you meet

The professionals that you meet will depend on your individual child's needs. You are, however, likely to meet a range of professionals from the health and education services and possibly also from social care and voluntary organisations.

It is important that you are aware of the role of each professional you're in contact with. If you are in any doubt, ask when you meet with them what their role involves and how they can support you and your child.

Parents as partners

It is very important that parents are viewed as partners when working with professionals. You are the expert on your own child, you live with your child 24 hours a day, seven days a week, you know them better than anybody else. The professionals are the experts in their specific field. For example, a teacher is a specialist in the field of education, and a physiotherapist is an expert in gross motor skills. If you are able to combine your expertise regarding your child and the professional's expertise, you can ensure that your child accesses the best provision to meet their needs.

At times, meeting with professionals can seem very daunting. Remembering that you are an expert about your child can help you to feel more confident.

Attending meetings

While we were writing this book, parents told us that that they often have to attend meetings to discuss their child's needs. It is important that you are aware of why the meeting is necessary and what is going to be discussed, as this will help you to feel more in control and to consider what you hope to gain from the meeting.

Before attending the meeting, ensure that you have the following information:

- What is the aim of the meeting?
- Who will be present?
- Where will the meeting be held?
- How long will the meeting last?

If you find repeating information about your child at every meeting is a strain, Down's Syndrome Association information officer, Susannah Seyman, advises: 'I know families who have created books about their children so all their information is in one place. There is a book like this in the Early Support Programme. You can write down everything – from your child's likes and dislikes to their medical information. It will save you from having to repeat things to different professionals.'

Location

Professionals are aware of the difficulty that some families have with attending meetings. If travelling is difficult, you may wish to suggest that the meeting be held in your own home. Consider whether you would feel more comfortable in your familiar surroundings. If you do decide to hold meetings in your own home, you may wish to follow these tips:

- Turn the television off so that there aren't any distractions.
- Don't feel that you have to provide refreshments, it will not be expected.
- Try to ensure that you aren't disturbed for the duration of the meeting. You may wish to consider turning your telephone off and forewarning friends that you will be busy during this time.
- Find out the number of professionals that are to attend in order to ensure that there will be enough space.

- Ask whether your child needs to be present at the meeting. If so, provide plenty of toys and activities so that you can concentrate on what is being said. Or ask a supportive friend if they would join you to keep your child occupied so that you can focus on the meeting.

Nina is a pre-school visiting teacher and often carries out visits in the home. She says: 'Families can feel more comfortable having meetings in their own home. It can help them to feel more relaxed and take the stress out of travelling to appointments. These meetings can work really well for both the professional and the parents.'

The meeting

It is helpful to take a little time prior to attending any meeting to consider whether there are any questions that you wish to ask or issues that need to be raised. Karon reminds us:

'The professionals are there to help you and your child. Be calm and polite, and be direct about what you want. I find it helps to write things down beforehand, particularly for paediatrician visits where there can be months between appointments. I write down all the little things that have occurred to me between appointments and then go through and ask them.'

Before a meeting consider the following points. You may want to talk these through with your partner or find a supportive friend:

- After finding out who will be present at the meeting, you should consider whether you have any specific questions for the professionals that are present.

- What do you hope to achieve from the meeting?

- Are there any issues that have been concerning you and that you would like to raise?

- You may find it helpful to write notes prior to attending the meeting. You can then refer to them to remind you about what you want to say.

- If you do not know some of the people present, ask that they introduce themselves and describe their role.

- Establish at the end of the meeting who will be carrying out which actions and by when.

> Families can feel more comfortable having meetings in their own home. It can help them to feel more relaxed and take the stress out of travelling to appointments. These meetings can work really well for both the professional and the parents.

- If another meeting is necessary, it is a good idea to request that a date is set while you have all of the professionals together. Getting numerous professionals to co-ordinate their diaries at a later date can prove to be difficult.

Olivia advises other parents to: 'Ask for copies of all the notes they write about your child, and keep a file. When it comes to meetings, make sure that you are prepared and ask questions. In my experience, professionals will tell you as little as possible if they think you won't understand or are not interested. The more you understand and the more interested you are, the more they will be willing to explain things to you. While you are at the appointment, you need to have your questions answered.'

More help

Making meetings easier

You may wish to follow these tips to help make working with professionals easier:

- Buy a family calendar and enter all appointments on it as soon as you receive them.

- Purchase an A4 file to keep a copy of all letters and reports that you receive. Taking this file to the meeting will ensure that you have all the information about your child to hand.

- If you have a partner and they cannot make the meeting, request a different appointment. If this is not possible, you could ask to record the meeting using a dictaphone so that your partner can hear exactly what is said.

- If your partner cannot make the meeting, you may wish to consider asking the professionals for their contact numbers so that your partner can contact them directly to ask any questions that they may have.

- If you are both attending the meeting, you may wish to discuss who is going to say what. One of you may feel more confident with speaking at these meetings than the other.

- Early Support was discussed in chapter 3. While it is intended for use with families of pre-school children, the materials can be extremely useful for all families. The Early Support materials include the use of a 'Family File'. This file provides a template for parents to share information with professionals. This includes information around issues such as the diagnosis which parents may find traumatic to keep relaying. The file also contains a template for an action plan which can be helpful to use in order to ascertain which professional is responsible for what role. Families can order the family pack from the Early Support website, contact details can be found in the help list.

Lisa has an eight month old son with Down's syndrome and advises: 'Make notes as soon as you get home or else every appointment blurs into one.'

Quick action checklist

This chapter has highlighted the number of professionals that you may meet when your child has Down's syndrome. You may want to:

- Take some time prior to meetings to think about what you hope to achieve and to make notes to help prompt you.

- Consider getting paperwork organised so that reports and appointment letters are always to hand.

Summing Up

Attending meetings can be hugely stressful. It is important that you spend some time considering what you want to gain from the meetings and that your voice is heard.

- Are you clear about who is involved with your child and what their roles are?

- Is there somebody that can support you at these meetings or are you confident attending alone?

- Have you organised the paperwork efficiently so that you can find reports quickly and easily?

Susannah Seyman, Down's Syndrome Association information officer, says: 'If you're not happy with a professional, do ask to change to someone else. You don't have to put up with someone you're not comfortable with.'

10

Moving Towards Adulthood

s your child grows older, he or she may want to become more independent. This can happen more slowly if your child has Down's syndrome and they may need more support. Growing independence is a challenging stage for both parent and young adult. In this chapter we look at supporting your child as they make friends, develop relationships, look for work and possibly move into a home of their own.

How to support your child

From age 14 onwards, your child can have important decisions to make about school, college or work and where to live. If your child has Down's syndrome, this can be a confusing time, and you may find it hard to navigate the different health and social care agencies involved. The 'Aiming High for Disabled Children: Better support for families' review found that more needed to be done to co-ordinate services for disabled young people in transition to adult life, and extra funding has been dedicated to ensure you and your child can access high quality information at key points.

Susannah Seyman, Down's Syndrome Association information officer, says: 'It can be very isolating when a young person with Down's syndrome moves on from children's services. To help reduce problems, work out with your child what they want in the future. The clearer you are about this, the easier it is to start fighting to get the services that you need to put your child's vision of their future in place.'

Valuing People Now is a government strategy for people with disabilities. It talks about 'transition' and what will happen to young people with disabilities around the time that they leave school. Planning at this stage should be 'person centred', which means that the professionals involved should listen to your child and help them to express their needs and desires and create plans to help them achieve these. If you feel that there are problems making the move from children's to adult's services for people with learning disabilities, you should contact your local director of social services who is responsible overall.

Your feelings about your child's independence

As a parent, you will have mixed feelings about your child's growing independence. It is a big step to let them take actions on their own for the first time and you may have concerns about the sort of support that they will receive.

Start planning your child's transition to adulthood early so your child has time to express their needs and adapt to change. This also gives you both a chance to check out all the options available and reassure yourself about the best ones for your child's circumstances.

Take time to listen to your teen's thoughts and desires. Find out about what they would like to do in the future and help them explain their wishes to professionals who work with you during this time of transition. The Foundation for People with Learning Disabilities offers a workbook called My Kind of Future to help your child plan their future, and offers parents' booklets called Prepared for the Future? and What Kind of a Future? Supporting young people with Down's syndrome to lead full lives after they leave school. Contact details can be found in the help list.

Encouraging hobbies and interests

Your child with Down's syndrome will have their own likes and dislikes. As time goes by, help them to express their preferences and choose activities that they like to do. Look for local clubs that they can join. This will help them get to know a wider range of people and try out different activities. You might have something like Guides or Scouts locally, a good youth club or a club specifically for young people with special needs or learning difficulties. Contact a Family has details of various local clubs (see help list).

Mencap runs the Gateway Award, an award scheme for young people aged 13 and over which encourages involvement in a range of activities and gives the chance to win awards for taking part.

See chapter 6 for information about a short break scheme too.

Education or employment

If your child is happily settled at a school, they may have the option to stay on after 16. For many though, as 16 approaches there are choices to be made. Ask your child's school about 'transition planning' at an early stage. Your child should be given a 'transition social worker' to help them.

The school should invite you in for a meeting about transition in Year 9 at around age 14. This meeting and the transition process should involve:

- A transition social worker.

- A local GP or community nurse.

- Teachers.

- Someone from the Connexions Service in England or Career Wales.

- An educational psychologist to help your child get the support they need to continue learning.

The process is similar in Northern Ireland. In Scotland, education authorities and schools have to meet certain timescales for planning, so 12 months before leaving school your child should have information from all the agencies that might be involved in their future. Six months before leaving school all the information on what your child needs should be passed onto the relevant agencies.

In England, the Connexions service provides careers information and advice and is available for young disabled people between the ages of 13 and 24 years. The Connexions adviser can advise about how your child can use adult services and decisions about funding further training. Contact your local Connexions adviser via your local Jobcentre Plus.

Going to college

Your local mainstream college may offer life skills courses, linked into level one literacy and numeracy. If your local college cannot offer a course to suit your child's disability-related needs, the Learning and Skills Council (LSC) may consider funding a place for your child at another more suitable college.

Your child will need to apply for college several months before leaving school – find out the specific dates for your area and choice of college. Visit the college and ask to meet the person responsible for helping students with additional needs. Talk to them about the sort of help your child might need. If they have one, look at their Statement of Special Educational Needs for details of the help they are getting.

Before your child signs up for a further education college course, the college should draw up a learning agreement setting out what they expect your child to do and how the college is going to help.

You can get help to find out about independent specialist colleges that provide further education or training for learners with learning difficulties and/or disabilities from the National Association of Specialist Colleges (Natspec). You can find details about how to contact them from their directory of colleges in the help list, or use the directory online at www.natspec.org.uk. This lists colleges by area and also allows you to search by the colleges' specialities.

Day centres

One option which may be available in your area is a place at a day centre for your child. At a day centre your child would get the chance to try various activities; however, many day centres have closed and young people are less likely to be offered a place. If there is a day centre available to your child, you should visit it to find out about the sort of activities available and whether the centre will provide help and training that will lead onto employment or education courses. Whether you are a carer or a parent, ask their teacher or social worker about what day centres are available in your locality.

In some areas, day centres are being replaced by services to help young people with learning disabilities to get out and take part in activities in the community. If your child gets direct payments, they can use these to pay for someone to help them access activities.

Funding and benefits while studying

If you live in England, Wales and Northern Ireland, people under the age of 19 get free further education. From 19 to 25, it depends on their benefits. In Scotland, it is free up to the age of 25. Your child may be eligible for Income Support and Housing Benefit while on courses if they usually get the disability element of those benefits

Learner Support Funds help students to overcome individual financial barriers to participating in learning. These funds are aimed at those in greatest need and colleges prioritise people with disabilities. The funds can be used to help with the cost of transport, childcare, residential lodgings and course related costs such as books, materials and equipment. You should contact the student support officer at the college concerned.

Developing independence and life skills

Supporting your child to become more independent is something that has to be done at the pace that is right for them. At home you can get your child involved with basic homecare to help them develop the skills they would need if they were to live independently in the future.

As one example, start talking about doing the washing when your child is in their early teens so they have time to get to grips with this basic life skill. Talk about cooking, healthy eating and choosing the right balance of food to stay healthy.

The tasks you share with your child will depend on their abilities and interest. Take some time to identify where your teenager could get more involved at home.

At 16, the rules change for DLA. If your child was not previously entitled to it, they should make a new claim as they may now qualify. From 16, a person does not need to show that they need more care or supervision than another person of the same age, which can mean that your child can now get the benefit at a higher rate. The allowance can now be paid directly to your child, or to another person who manages their money. See chapter 8 for more about finance and benefits. If your child remains in full-time education, you should continue to claim Child Benefit.

Finding a home

At some point you and your child may feel that it is right for them to live more independently. Susannah Seyman of the Down's Syndrome Association says: 'People with Down's syndrome want to leave home just as much as their siblings. They may leave in their early- to mid-20s, a few years later than siblings.'

You should contact the local council to find out about the options in your area. There may be sheltered housing or supported living schemes that are appropriate. You can plan for your child to learn skills to move towards independent living at a time that is right for them.

Health

Your child will need to move from children's health services to adult health services at some point. Talk to the professionals involved about doing this in a gradual way at the appropriate time. You can ask for a meeting with the professionals involved for a proper handover.

The Transition Information Network is a website for parents, carers and people who work with and for disabled young people in transition to adulthood. It offers a magazine, e-newsletter and seminars.

Finding work

It is harder for anyone with a disability to find the right sort of work; around half of people with a disability are employed and this drops to around 10% of those with a learning disability. Your local Jobcentre Plus can put you in touch with a disability employment adviser, who will help to work out the sort of employment or training that will suit your child. They can also help with a referral to Work Preparation, an individually tailored programme designed to help some disabled people, or to a work programme like the Job Introduction Scheme, WORKSTEP or Access to Work. If your child is 16 or older and has left school, they may be entitled to Employment and Support Allowance, although this can affect your entitlement to other benefits.

The Shaw Trust works with people who have a disability but want to work. They offer activities that can help individuals develop the skills they need to be 'work ready' and that will help them to live independently. The trust also offers personal development and training courses to help your child decide where they want to be and to equip them with the skills and motivation to get there, as well as programmes to help them move from benefits into employment (see help list).

Celebrating success

Learning to be proud of what they achieve can help your child move happily into adult life. During this time of transition remember to take time to celebrate. If you and your child attend a transition meeting at school, take time together afterwards to talk about what went well. Help them celebrate leaving school, getting onto a placement scheme, finding work or a place to live.

Quick action checklist

- Talk to your child about their aims and ideas for the next few years.
- Talk to their school to find out about the transition meeting.
- Check if your child's benefits are likely to change.

Summing Up

As your child with Down's syndrome reaches the age of 14, they should be offered help to make decisions about their own future. It can take time and support from a number of professionals to help your child work out what they want and put the support in place to allow them to gradually become more independent. If you are not offered help, speak to your child's school or social worker about what is on offer in your area.

It may be helpful to speak to other parents about their experiences around transition. Many parents have positive stories to share, which can help you to feel better about the changes ahead. While this period may seem daunting, it can also be an exciting time for both you and your child.

Help List

Advisory Centre for Education (ACE Centre)
Address: ACE Education Advice & Training, 72 Durnsford Road, London N11 2EJ
Tel: 0300 0115 142
Email: enquiries@ace-ed.org.uk
Website: www.ace-ed.org.uk
Info: Provides information about state education in England and Wales for children aged five to 16, with telephone advice on special educational needs matters.

British Institute of Learning Disabilities (BILD)
Address: BILD Birmingham Research Park, 97 Vincent Drive, Edgbaston, Birmingham, B15 2SQ
Tel: 0121 415 6960
Email: enquiries@bild.org.uk
Website: www.bild.org.uk
Info: Body that works to improve the lives of people with disabilities. Provides a range of published and online information.

Contact a Family
Address: 209-211 City Road, London, EC1V 1JN
Tel: 0808 808 3555 (helpline, Monday to Friday, 10am-4pm)
Email: info@cafamily.org.uk
Website: www.cafamily.org.uk
Info: Provides advice, information and support for families with disabled children.

Council for Disabled Children
Address: National Children's Bureau, 8 Wakley Street, London, EC1V 7QE
Tel: 020 7843 1900
Email: cdc@ncb.org.uk
Website: https://councilfordisabledchildren.org.uk/
Info: The Council for Disabled Children are an umbrella organisation of UK charities for the welfare of disabled children, with over 250 member organisations.

Disability Living Allowance (DLA)
Website: https://www.gov.uk/browse/disabilities
Info: Find out if you are entitled to the DLA benefits scheme.

Down's Syndrome Association

Address: Langdon Down Centre, 2a Langdon Park, Teddington, Middlesex, TW11 9PS
Tel: 0333 1212 300
Email: info@downs-syndrome.org.uk
Website: http://www.downs-syndrome.org.uk/
Info: Provides information and support for people with Down's syndrome, their families and carers.

Down's Syndrome Education International

Address: 6 Underley Business Centre, Kirkby, Lonsdale, Cumbria, LA6 2DY UK
Tel: 0330 043 0021
Email: hello@dseinternational.org
Website: https://www.dseinternational.org
Info: Down Syndrome Education International undertakes research and provides advice and support to families, teachers, therapists and other professionals across the UK.

Family Fund

Address: 4 Alpha Court, Monks Cross Drive, York, YO32 9WN
Tel: 01904 550055
Website: https://www.familyfund.org.uk
Info: The Family Fund helps families with severely disabled children to have choices and the opportunity to enjoy ordinary life. Contact the organisation for grants and funding information.

Mencap

Address: Royal Mencap Society, Mencap National Centre, 123 Golden Lane,
London EC1Y 0RT
Tel: 0808 808 1111
Email: helpline@mencap.org.uk
Website: https://www.mencap.org.uk
Info: Mencap works with and for people with learning disabilities, their families and carers. They offer a list of solicitors who have a specialist interest in creating wills that provide for the future of someone with a learning disability.

Mosaic Down Syndrome UK

Email: Judy.Green@blueyonder.co.uk; Bill.Green@blueyonder.co.uk
Website: http://www.mosaicdownsyndrome.org/
Info: A support group for parents of children with Mosaic Down Syndrome.

Sibs

Address: Meadow Field, Stell Hill, Keighley BD22 9JD
Tel: 01535 645453
Contact form: https://www.sibs.org.uk/contact/
Website: https://www.sibs.org.uk
Info: Provides support for people who have a disabled brother or sister.

Special Kids in the UK

Address: Special Kids in the UK, PO Box 1225, Enfield, EN1 9TH
Tel: 07876 796 453
Email: information@specialkidsintheuk.org
Website: http://specialkidsintheuk.org/
Info: A charity set up by parents to support parents. Includes an online forum that is a great place to share information and gain support.

The Down's Heart Group

Address: PO Box 4260, Dunstable, LU6 2ZT
Tel: 0300 102 1644
Email: info@dhg.org.uk
Website: www.dhg.org.uk
Info: Offers support and contact between families.
It encourages research into heart defects, publishes a newsletter and has a wide range of information available, details on request.

The Down's Syndrome Medical Interest Group

Address: Down Syndrome Medical Interest Group, The Children's Development Centre, City Hospital Campus, Nottingham, NG5 1PB
Tel: 0115 88 31158
Email: info@dsmig.org.uk
Website: http://www.dsmig.org.uk/
Info: Provides essential information for healthcare professionals on 'best practice' medical care for people with Down's syndrome in the UK and Ireland.

The Shaw Trust

Address: Shaw Trust, Third Floor, 10 Victoria Street, Bristol, BS1 6BN
Tel: 0345 234 9675
Email: support@shaw-trust.org.uk
Website: www.shaw-trust.org.uk
Info: A national charity which supports disabled and disadvantaged people to prepare for work, find jobs and live more independently.

Book List

Abortion – The Essential Guide
By Johanna Payton, Need2Know, Peterborough, 2009

Don't Let It Get You Down Syndrome
By SK Dinning, Createspace, USA, 2014

Down Syndrome: The Facts
By Mark Selikowitz, OUP, Oxford, 2008

Insomnia – The Essential Guide
By Antonia Chitty & Victoria Dawson, Peterborough, 2009

My Friend Has Down's Syndrome (Let's Talk About It!)
By Jennifer Moore-Mallinos, Barron's Educational Series, Hauppauge USA, 2009

Pregnancy: Older Women – The Essential Guide
By Jo Johnson, Peterborough, 2009

Special Educational Needs – A Parent's Guide
By Antonia Chitty & Victoria Dawson, Peterborough, 2008

Stress – The Essential Guide
By Frances Ive, Peterborough, 2008

Supporting Positive Behavior in Children and Teens with Down Syndrome: The Respond but Don't React Method
By David Stein, Woodbine House Inc., Bethesda MD USA, 2016

Whole Child Reading: A Quick-Start Guide to Teaching Students with Down Syndrome & Other Developmental Delays
By Natalie Hale, Woodbine House, Bethesda MD USA, 2016